The Way of Wisdom

For Kirstin and Paul
On the threshold of all your tomorrows

THE WAY OF
Wisdom

Margaret Silf

LION

Copyright © 2006 Margaret Silf

The author asserts the moral right
to be identified as the author of this work

A Lion Book
an imprint of
Lion Hudson plc
Mayfield House, 256 Banbury Road,
Oxford OX2 7DH, England
www.lionhudson.com
ISBN 978 0 7459 5210 9
ISBN 0 7459 5210 0

First edition 2006
10 9 8 7 6 5 4 3 2 1 0

Frontispiece illustration by Renée Jepson

A catalogue record for this book is available
from the British Library

The text paper used in this book has been made
from wood independently certified as having come
from sustainable forests.

Typeset in 12/15 BerkeleyOldStyle
Printed and bound in Great Britain
by Cox & Wyman Ltd

Contents

Introduction

How do we make our way wisely in this increasingly
complex world, where the paths we walk seem so often
to tie us in knots, and lead us round in circles?

How do we discover that elusive 'pearl of wisdom',
of which we speak in proverb and in prayer?

Is wisdom something that only a very favoured few can
ever attain, or is it actually all around us, like ripe but
invisible fruit, just waiting to be gathered, and shared?

When I was asked to compile this anthology of wisdom
writings, my reaction was twofold. There was delight, at the
prospect of exploring so many potentially rich sources of
wisdom, but also dismay at the impossibility of ever
drawing together a collection that even remotely represents
the infinity of wisdom – human and divine – that lies all
around us, among us, and within us.

The result is merely a taster of all that might be. But,
more than that, it is an invitation to you to explore the
ways of wisdom for yourself. It invites you to ponder the
wisdom that runs like a golden thread through the story
of our universe, through the created world around us, and
through the intuitions of our early forebears and their still
living traditions. It calls to you to gather wisdom from your
own desert experiences, as well as from your happier
memories. May it remind you that wisdom grows and
flourishes both in times when the signposts are clear, and

also when the clouds are down. In short, this book invites you to embrace and to celebrate the wisdom that your own life and your own heart are yielding.

Experience is the seed of wisdom, and we all have experience. None is excluded from the 'university of life', where heart-wisdom, not head-knowledge, is learned. But the seeds of wisdom that life sows in our hearts and memories need to be cared for, watered and nourished, and we do this when we take time to *reflect* on our experience. This book invites you to enter into this reflective process, and discover what those seeds are becoming for you.

And where does the way of wisdom lead? To the deep centre of who we are, perhaps. There to discover the ground of our being, whom many would call 'God', and to recognize the deep centre of each other, calling us into a mutual respect that alone will take us beyond the defensive and adversarial instincts that hold us captive in conflict and distrust.

The way of wisdom is for roaming and browsing. It can never be fenced in, nor will it ever be fully known, mapped and defined, and this is the joy of it. There is always more and more to discover and to share, because every new day opens up new pathways to explore. And this 'more' is for sharing, and for living. When we live from the centre of wisdom in our hearts, we can no longer live only for ourselves, for wisdom is the golden thread that binds heart to heart, and reminds us moment by moment that in the heart of God we are all one, and each one is uniquely cherished.

I wish you continuing joy in the ongoing exploration of your own heart's wisdom and the recognition of the wisdom that dwells in the hearts of others. Thank you for allowing me to journey these sacred ways with you for a while. And a special thank you to Morag Reeve, of Lion Hudson, for inviting me to write this book, and for all her personal support, encouragement and guiding wisdom along the way; to Liz Evans and Catherine Giddings for editing the text with such care and sensitivity; to Renée Jepson for her kind permission to reproduce her 'owl of wisdom'; and to all those wise ones – men, women and children – who have shared their wisdom with me through my life, often without ever knowing that they were doing so. I thank them all, in the words of Dag Hammarskjöld:

For all that has been, thanks! For all that shall be, yes!

Original Wisdom

'In the beginning…' This is how the story starts.
'Once upon a time…' This is how so many stories begin.

But the story we are about to explore is the story that contains, and inspires, all the other stories. It is the sacred story of who we are, what our existence means, and how it came to be. This is the story in which eternal mystery and personal history meet and embrace.

For those of us who inhabit the twenty-first century, the call to return to 'the beginning' is an invitation into a very long journey indeed. By today's reckoning, our universe is up to fifteen billion years old, and when we get back to the beginning, we hit a brick wall at which the laws of physics break down, and the human intellect can go no further.

Once upon a time…

'Once upon a time' carries us right back in time until we arrive at the point at which there is no 'before' – the point at

---

**The day of my awakening was the day I saw and knew I saw
all things in God and God in all things.**
Mechtild of Magdeburg

which both time and space, or, as we know it now, space-time, has its genesis.

And what do we find there? Is it the vast void we may have imagined? Is it the Big Bang that set a universe in motion? And the most searching questions of all: is it personal? Is it wise? Is it love? Is it God? The author of John's Gospel expresses this sense of a life-giving, loving, creative presence that has been in creation from the beginning, and continues to reveal itself in time and space.

In the beginning was the Word,
the Word was with God,
and the Word was God.
He was with God in the beginning.
Through him all things came into being,
Not one thing came into being except through him.
What has come into being in him was life,
Life that was the light of men;
And light shines in darkness,
And darkness could not overpower it.
John 1:1–5

What Word is this, who reverberates through the aeons of the sacred story? For John, he is the Logos, the Word in whom the profoundest wisdom is vested, from which all creation will unfurl itself. Our own words are helpless to describe these mysteries, and yet in our own words and silences we strive for a glimpse of this deep, foundational

---

Here in its human mode, the universe reflects on and celebrates itself in a unique mode of conscious self-awareness.
Thomas Berry

wisdom, and when we encounter it, our hearts leap in recognition.

> *The human word is only one among billions of words that*
> *God has spoken and that therefore emanate from the divine*
> *splendour. To make contact with wisdom is to go beyond*
> *human words, which have, after all, existed for only about*
> *four million years – and have appeared on paper for only*
> *a few thousand years and in print for only five hundred.*
> Matthew Fox[1]

The biblical writers seem to be in agreement that wisdom is a creating force that has characterized and shaped the unfolding universe from its very beginnings, and continues to shape and form human minds and hearts through all the ages.

The writer of Proverbs, for example, imagines wisdom as the eternal playmate of the creator, alongside God from the very beginning, the first fruit of the mind of God:

> *Yahweh created me, first-fruits of his fashioning,*
>   *before the oldest of his works.*
> *From everlasting, I was firmly set,*
> *From the beginning, before the earth came into being.*
> *The deep was not, when I was born,*
> *Nor were the springs with their abounding waters.*
> *Before the mountains were settled,*
> *Before the hills, I came to birth;*

You think because you understand one you must also
understand two, because one and one make two.

Before he had made the earth, the countryside and
  the first elements of the world.
When he fixed the heavens firm, I was there,
When he drew a circle on the surface of the deep,
When he thickened the clouds above,
When the sources of the deep began to swell,
When he assigned the sea its boundaries
when he traced the foundations of the earth,
I was beside the master craftsman,
Delighting him day after day,
Ever at play in his presence,
At play everywhere on his earth,
Delighting to be with the children of men.
Proverbs 8:22–31

Some of today's scientific minds are no less poetic when
they seek to describe the beginnings of our universe. I
remember being startled to see a poster above the desk of
an astrophysicist working in a university observatory, which
announced that 'We are made of stardust!' It wasn't the
kind of exuberant language I would have expected a
scientist to endorse. Yet as the course I was there to attend
progressed, I learned for myself just how literally true this
statement is. The elements of our own bodies are made of
the same elements that were scattered into space in the
brilliant supernova death of a star that existed billions of
years ago. We are made of stardust, and shaped and
energized by that same pulsing power and unfathomable

But you must also understand 'and'.
Jelaluddin Rumi

wisdom that brought a universe into being. This is a statement of fact, as well as a statement of faith. In both the ancient seers and modern physicists, there is the same sense of a connection, an intimate relationship, between the visible world and an invisible, but all-powerful wisdom and power that shapes it and forms it.

> *Originating power brought forth a universe. All the energy that would ever exist in the entire course of time erupted as a single quantum – a singular gift – existence. If in the future, stars would blaze and lizards would blink in their light, these actions would be powered by the same numinous energy that flared forth at the dawn of time.*
>
> *There was no place in the universe that was separate from the originating power of the universe. Each thing of the universe had its very roots in this realm. Even space-time itself was a tossing, churning, foaming out of the originating reality, instant by instant. Each of the sextillion particles that foamed into existence had its root in this quantum vacuum, this originating reality…*
>
> *In the beginning space foamed forth to create the vast billowing event of the expanding universe. The universe venture was under way.*
>
> **Brian Swimme and Thomas Berry**[2]

The universe venture
As long as human beings have walked this planet, we have

Creation is an ongoing process, a continual becoming.
Robert Fripp

asked ourselves the big question: did this universe 'just happen' or is it the expression of some Wisdom far beyond anything our finite minds could grasp?

I well remember the night I watched a documentary programme that revealed to me for the first time the awesome unfolding of our universe over fifteen billion years. The sheer scale of the story took my breath away. I felt as though my mind had been liberated from a cage, and I realized that anything humankind could ever think or express of this mystery would always be far too small to hold the wonder of it.

Over the centuries, many metaphors have been used in the attempt to express the logic that underpins creation. We are just emerging from the age of the 'watchmaker' metaphor, when it was widely held that God, the watchmaker, designed creation, and then somehow set it going. After that it just carried on working (more or less to plan) without further intervention. This led us to believe that if the universe is some vast machine, some great feat of divine precision engineering, then if we could understand all its component parts, we would understand the whole – we would (and here we can only gasp at our own temerity) 'understand the mind of God'.

This metaphor has moved on dramatically in our own generation. Now we are more likely to try to grasp at the mystery in terms of an unfolding, and still emerging *process*. Where that process is going is something we cannot know, and yet we are active participants in it. It matters, how we

---

**Wisdom is encoded in the very stuff on which it must act,
the blueprint and the builder all in one.**
Gerald Schroeder

live and love and make our choices. The wisdom that underpins creation also energizes and shapes our own minds and hearts. There is a direct relationship, and an unbroken link, between the first flaring forth of the universe and the molecules of our own bodies. We are, quite literally, 'made of stardust'. The amazing variety of living forms has its genesis in this first beginning, where Wisdom was God's playmate and companion.

This seemingly modern notion is older than we might think. Augustine of Hippo is convinced that:

> *The universe was brought into being in a less than fully formed state, but was gifted with the capacity to transform itself from unformed matter into a truly marvellous array of structure and life forms.*
> **Augustine of Hippo[3]**

Gerald Schroeder echoes and expands on this conviction:

> *Our sun, the planets and we ourselves are the products of bygone stars that blasted their contents into space and reformed to make new generations of stars. We are stardust come alive, and somehow conscious of being alive.*
>
> *A single consciousness, an all-encompassing wisdom, pervades the universe. The discoveries of science, those that search the quantum nature of subatomic matter, those that explore the molecular complexity of biology, and those that probe the brain/mind interface, have moved us to the brink*

Astronomers now trace our Earth's origins back to stars that died before the solar system formed.

of a startling realization: all existence is the expression
of this wisdom. In the laboratories we experience it as
information first physically articulated as energy and then
condensed into the form of matter. Every particle, every
being, from atom to human, appears to have within it
a level of information, of conscious wisdom.

Somehow the dust spewed into space by the nuclear
furnace of a bygone supernova has become a human brain
that learned to make nuclear reactors here on earth.

Wisdom is encoded in the very stuff on which it must
act, the blueprint and the builder all in one.
Gerald Schroeder[4]

Recent theory suggests that between 13.5 and 15 billion
years ago the whole enormity of Creation derived from a
single point. Theory goes on to describe that once-and-
forever point as being greatly smaller than a proton, which
is itself a subcomponent of an atom in our given scheme
of things. (If an atom were the size of a football field, the
proton at its core would be smaller than the ball.) Everything
from nothing. To imagine such a feat comes as something of
a shock, yet that is precisely what two major religious
traditions have suggested all along.

Creation is an ongoing process, a continual becoming.
Robert Fripp[5]

And the Genesis writer reminds us that in the beginning,

These ancient stars made the atoms of which we
and our planet are composed.
Martin Rees

God proclaimed a resounding and unequivocal 'YES!' to the unfolding dream:

God saw all he had made,
and indeed it was very good.
Genesis 1:31

Matthew Fox expresses this 'yes' in terms of on ongoing, unending *blessing* of God upon all that God has made and of every part of creation upon every other part in a great chain of love:

If it is true that all creation flows from a single, loving
source, then all of creation is blessed and is a blessing,
atom to atom, molecule to molecule, organism to
organism, land to plants, plants to animals, animals to
other animals, people to people, and back to atoms,
molecules, plants, fishes.
Matthew Fox[6]

The unfolding logic

Not only did our universe emerge from a 'once-and-forever point' quite impossible to see, or measure or in any way comprehend, it also emerged with an elegance that defies imagination. Our distant ancestors could only intuit, in story and in ritual, the deep logic of creation, and their own sense of participating in a process that is perfectly and finely

---

We are stardust come alive, and somehow
conscious of being alive.
Gerald Schroeder

tuned to lead not just to life as we know it, but to
conscious life, capable of reflecting on its own source
and destiny. What they could only guess at, science now
confirms.

Martin Rees, a Nobel prize-winner and Astronomer
Royal, has analyzed what he calls 'just six numbers' which
determined the way the embryonic universe unfolded. Had
any one of these defining numbers been even marginally
different from what it was, no life as we know it would have
emerged in our universe.

*These six numbers constitute a 'recipe' for a universe.
Moreover, the outcome is sensitive to their values: if any
one of them were to be 'untuned', there would be no stars
and no life… It is astonishing that an expanding universe,
whose starting point is so 'simple' that it can be specified
by just a few numbers, can evolve (if these numbers are
suitably 'tuned') into our intricately structured cosmos.*

*All the atoms in the universe could result from a tiny bias
in favour of matter over anti-matter. We, and the visible
universe around us, may exist only because of a difference
in the ninth decimal place between the numbers of quarks
and antiquarks.*

*Ever since the beginning, gravity has been moulding
cosmic structures and enhancing temperature contrasts,
a prerequisite for the emergence of the complexity that lies
around us ten billion years later, and of which we are a part.*

Even this colossal universe, whose extent requires a

**If God had been indifferent to you,
he'd have made someone else.**
Ralph Wright OSB

million-digit number to express it, may not be 'everything there is'. It is the outcome of one episode of inflation, but that episode – that Big Bang – may itself just be one event in an infinite ensemble.
Martin Rees[7]

What wisdom is being made manifest in this fine-tuning? What guiding mind weaves this web of being into existence? For many earth-dwellers, whether they consider themselves 'religious' or not, the evidence points to something, or Someone, who not only reveals a supreme intellect, but also a deep desire for life, so much so that every factor in creation and every event that happens, becomes in these hands, a means towards ever more complex and differentiated life. And all of this potential was there in that first 'singularity', far too small for human observation, almost nothing, yet containing in potential everything that would ever become, including you and me, and every idea we would ever share.

We find a remarkable degree of ordering within the universe, which can be expressed concisely and elegantly in mathematical forms. The fact that so much of the deep structure of the universe can be represented mathematically points to something remarkable about both the universe itself and to the ability of the human mind to understand it. It is almost as if the human mind has been designed to grasp the patterns and structures of the cosmos.

Single-celled protozoans boast an architecture that is, as one observer put it, 'two billion years ahead of its time'.

The structure of the universe is determined by a series of 'fundamental constants' that shape its contours and development. Had these been different, the universe would have taken a very different form – and life, as we know it, could not have emerged. The fabric of the universe seems to have been designed to establish the possibility of life.
Alister McGrath[8]

The rate of spatial emergence reveals a primordial elegance. Had space unfurled in a more retarded fashion, the expanding universe would have collapsed back into quantum foam billions of years ago. Such a collapse would have taken place even if space had unfurled one trillionth of a percent more slowly. If space had emerged more rapidly, equally disastrous results would have followed.
Brian Swimme and Thomas Berry [9]

Such elegance is a very far cry indeed from the possibility that creation just came together as a result of random mutations and chance cosmic events. If we were to witness even the beginnings of such precise engineering in human achievement we would award it the highest acclaim. If we were to experience even a hint of such a lyrical outpouring of possibility from a human source, we would know that we were in the divine presence of the heart of a poet.

And in all this vastness, what about ourselves…?

The amoebas had the architectural ideas of R. Buckminster Fuller before there was anyone around capable of having an idea.
Matthew Fox

In such a universe, where am I?

When we gaze up on a starlit night, we may well feel so overawed by the enormity of space, and so mind-blown by the unimaginable distances, that we feel ourselves to be utterly insignificant. Some of the light we are seeing began its journey to our retinas millions of light years ago. We stand on a minor planet, gazing into space, and know that we occupy a place somewhere on the edge of a galaxy that is one among trillions of galaxies. Can it possibly matter what becomes of us? Who do we think we are?

Matthew Fox reminds us, if we need reminding, of the scale involved here and the minute proportion of cosmic time that has been associated with self-conscious human life, let alone organized religion:

> At our University of Creation Spirituality, one enters by ascending a staircase. On the left wall of that staircase we have painted a history of the universe. The mural is scientifically accurate as to the proportionate distance the universe has travelled and we travel when mounting the stairs. The Milky Way appears three-quarters up the steps. When does humanity appear? Well beyond the light switch at the top of the stairs! Humanity is accurately represented by a strip one-quarter of an inch wide at the very top of the stairs. Our religions would be a speck of dust in that quarter inch and our races, too, would be merely a speck of dust.
> **Matthew Fox**[10]

From the beginning till now the entire creation, as we know it, has been groaning in one great act of giving birth,

Many have asked these existential questions before us. Barbara Brown Taylor captures something of our response, even as she reflects our chaotic sense of somehow 'belonging' to this mystery, of being held in it, being in relationship with it.

When I look up at the stars there is a small commotion in my bones, as the ashes of dead stars that house my marrow rise up like metal filings toward the magnet of their living kin.

Where am I in this picture? I am all over the place. I am up there, down here, inside my skin and out. I am large compared to a virus and small compared to the sun, with a life permeable to them both. Am I alone? How could I ever be alone? I am part of a web that is pure relationship, with energy available to me that has been around since the universe was born.

Where is God in this picture? God is all over the place. God is up there, down here, inside my skin and out. God is the web, the energy, the space, the light – not captured in them, as if any of those concepts were more real than what unites them – but revealed in that singular, vast net of relationship that animates everything there is.

At this point in my thinking, it is not enough for me to proclaim that God is responsible for all this unity. Instead I want to proclaim that God is the unity – the very energy, the very intelligence, the very elegance and passion that make it all go. This is the God who is not somewhere but

---

**and not only creation but all of us who possess
the first-fruits of the Spirit.**
Romans 8:22–23

everywhere, the God who can be prayed to in all directions at once. This is also the God beyond all directions, who will still be here (wherever 'here' means) when the universe either dissipates into dust or swallows itself up again. Paul Tillich's name for this divine reality was 'the ground of all being'. The only thing I can think of that is better than that is the name God revealed to Moses: 'I am who I am.'... It sounds like the singular utterance of the only One who ever was, is, or shall be, in whom everything else abides. For the moment, we see through a glass darkly. We live in the illusion that we are all separate 'I ams'. When the fog finally clears, we shall know there is only One.

Barbara Brown Taylor[11]

I will never forget an experience I once had as a small girl. I was walking home from a Brownie meeting one November night, when something made me look up. What I saw transfixed me, and the vision is as vivid in my memory today as it was on the night it happened. It was one of those nights when the stars were so bright, and seemed so close, that you could have plucked them from the sky, like ripe silver apples from a laden tree. Although I couldn't have expressed at the time what I felt, now I would describe my feelings at that moment as twofold: I felt utterly alone in a vast, but breathtakingly beautiful universe, and yet at the same time utterly at home in it, and totally enfolded and cherished by it. Half a century later I was swept up by this same sense of mystery and belonging

---

A god who can be fashioned, a god who can be confined, is but a shadow of man.
Abraham Joshua Heschel

while on a tiny island on the Great Barrier Reef, seventy kilometres east of the Queensland coast in Australia. There, standing on the island's helipad late at night, I gazed up at the brilliance of the southern skies as once I had marvelled at the starlit skies above my childhood home. That night a number of astrophysicists were also present on the helipad. They were taking a break after a scientific conference in Sydney, and it was obvious that they were experiencing the same sense of wonder and mystery. We gazed together, in silent awe.

In both these sacred moments of my own story, I was touched by that deep sense of 'oneness' with creation that Barbara Brown Taylor describes, and many 'mystics', both ordinary and extraordinary, have echoed.

It took all the chemistry
since Big Bang
to pedigree
the DNA
union
that is 'me'

that's one
huge
mind-defying
History
– Heap Big Mystery

All know that the drop merges into the ocean but few know that the ocean merges into the drop.
Kabir (Sufi mystic)

the answer to all harmony is seeing
that this is not just inconceivable
but true

and for 'you' too!
Ralph Wright[12]

We are more than human beings, we are cosmic beings,
'formed from stardust', and when we catch a glimpse of this
deeper belonging, we suddenly feel 'at home' in the universe,
and we desire to work for the good of the whole, rather than
strive only to satisfy the part. The paradox of spirituality is
that in serving the whole the part is truly satisfied. This is
the testimony of saints and martyrs throughout history, and
we can experience this for ourselves today.
David Tacey[13]

We belong, not merely to the created order of things, but
in a great web of relationship, and interconnectedness, in
which every particle is intimately interwoven with every
other, and in which, in some mysterious way, each particle
holds and reflects something of the totality. This makes a
huge difference to the way we live. Every choice we make,
every response we offer, every reaction we reveal has an
effect on that web of being. We are made for relationship.
The Wisdom of creation insists on it. No single creature can
disengage from the dance of creation without jeopardizing
the eternal beauty of that dance. We are indeed created to

Stop talking, stop thinking, and there is nothing you will not
understand. Return to the Root and you will find the Meaning.
Seng-ts'an/sosan

be 'we'. To opt for merely being 'I' is to opt out of the creative process itself. It is only in interrelationship that we have our being and our meaning.

Now we're learning from the new sciences that the universe has actually been constructed as a We. Everything in creation – oceans, whales, mountains, humans, eagles, roses, giraffes and viruses – is a dance of subatomic particles. Fields of energy flow and mingle together. They are all stitched into the cosmic quilt which underlies and gives rise to everything.

In every particle, there is God, weaving the 'cosmic quilt' from the fibres of divine wisdom. God is in all things and all things are in God.
Sue Monk Kidd[14]

The whole in every part

There is an abundance, and a superabundance in creation that defies all reason. The Big Bang thrusts forth the raw materials of trillions of galaxies, each with billions of stars. Earth brings forth an over-the-top harvest of seed and fruit, in the hope that the odd one here and there will grow into the new generation. God 'thinks big', bigger than any human mind can comprehend. God creates in utterly unreasonable measure. God flings out the miles while we count the inches.

If we could really take hold of the magnitude of the

Wisdom includes the universe and wisdom passes through the heart.
Matthew Fox

universe venture, what difference would it make to our living and our praying?

> *If we could actually feel ourselves sliding through space at the rate of six hundred thirty kilometres per second, would we still pester God about good weather for the family reunion or the new members' drive at church?*
> **Barbara Brown Taylor**[15]

Annie Dillard captures a sense of the superabundance of creation, while the fourteenth-century English mystic Dame Julian of Norwich sees the whole in the tiniest part:

> *Extravagant gesture is the very stuff of creation. After one extravagant gesture of creation in the first place, the universe has continued to deal exclusively in extravagances, flinging intricacies and colossi down aeons of emptiness, heaping profusions on profligacies with ever-fresh vigour. The whole show has been on fire from the word go. I come down to the water to cool my eyes. But everywhere I look I see fire; that which isn't flint is tinder, and the whole world sparks and flames.*
> **Annie Dillard**[16]

> *He showed me a little thing, the size of a hazelnut, in the palm of my hand, and it was as round as a ball. I looked at it with my mind's eye and I thought, 'What can this be?' And the answer came, 'It is all that is made.' I marvelled*

When order crumbles, mystery rises.
John Shea

that it could last, for I thought it might have crumbled to nothing, it was so small. And the answer came into my mind, 'It lasts and ever shall because God loves it.' And all things have being through the love of God.

In this little thing I saw three truths. The first is that God made it. The second is that God loves it. The third is that God looks after it.

Julian of Norwich[17]

And an image from the Upanishads draws together the macrocosm of an immeasurable universe and the microcosm of a human heart seeking to reflect on the wonder of it all:

In the body there is a little shrine.
In that shrine there is a lotus.
In that lotus there is a little space.
What is it that lives in that little space?
The whole universe is in that little space,
Because the creator,
The source of it all,
Is in the heart of each one of us.
Parable from the Upanishads

The wisdom that goes through the heart

The image of an axis is very familiar to us, from the simple astronomy we learn in school. The earth spins about its axis

---

We are more than human beings, we are cosmic beings.
David Tacey

and this in turn holds the times and seasons in balance and determines the interchange of night and day. There is a sense that when we are spinning around the true axis, all will be held in its true balance, and the rightness of life will be maintained.

But what if this 'true axis' were also to pass through our own hearts. Is it not so, that we know, in the core of our being, when we are being true to the best in ourselves and when we are 'off course'? We have a sense that our inner axis is somehow tilted, and that our responses to the challenges of life are often distorted. Yet we also know when the deep wisdom of which we are but one small manifestation, is running true. These are the moments when we recognize the touch of God in ourselves and in each other, and we long for these glimpses to be fulfilled.

It is evident that in all teachings of wisdom, wisdom includes the universe and wisdom passes through the heart. Wisdom is knowledge and awareness and experience of the whole that touches the heart. Many traditions honour the special place where heart and universe, microcosm and macrocosm, meet.
Matthew Fox[18]

The profound connection between our own hearts and the wisdom of the universe brings the real challenge of our living. If we imagine the original Wisdom, the Wisdom of God, as the source and the emergence of a cosmic Dream

---

Every one of us will change the world, whether we mean to or not.
Barbara Brown Taylor

of life, then we have a part to play in the fulfilling of that Dream, in making it enfleshed and incarnate in our own personal circumstances on planet earth.

> *The archetypal journey of the universe can now be experienced as the journey of each individual, since the entire universe has been involved in shaping our individual psychic as well as our physical being from that first awesome moment when the universe emerged.*
>
> *The most appropriate way of describing this process seems to be that of dream realisation. The universe seems to be the fulfilment of something so highly imaginative and so overwhelming that it must have been dreamed into existence.*
>
> **Thomas Berry**[19]

Ronald Rohlheiser, in his Internet reflections for Lent 2005, reminds us that this Dream has been within us not only since the day we were born, but since the very beginning, when the molecules that shape us were being fashioned among the stars, and the energy that gives us life and meaning was flaring forth from the very heart of God:

> *Ancient philosophers and mystics used to say that, before being born, each soul is kissed by God and then goes through life always, in some dark way, remembering that kiss and measuring everything in relation to its original sweetness.*

On a clear night, for every star we see, there are 50 million more behind it.
Margaret Wheatley

Inside each of us, there is a dark memory of having once
been touched and caressed by hands far gentler than our
own. That caress has left a permanent imprint inside us,
one so tender and good that its memory becomes a prism
through which we see everything else.

Thus we recognize love and truth outside of us precisely
because they resonate with something that is already inside
us. Things 'touch our hearts' because they awaken a
memory of that original kiss. Moreover, because we have
a memory of once having been perfectly touched, caressed,
and loved, every experience we meet in life falls a little
short. We have already had something deeper. When we feel
frustrated, angry, betrayed, violated, or enraged it is because
our outside experience does not honour what we already
know and cling to inside.

Ronald Rohlheiser [20]

To be a part of this unfolding Dream is at once an
awesome responsibility and an amazing privilege. It means
that every choice we make, every relationship we share,
every reaction and response, the life-changing decisions
and the momentary gestures alike, have the potential to
make a difference to the way in which the divine wisdom
finds expression on planet earth. The inner awareness of
this wisdom, this baptism in love, described by Rohlheiser,
is our infallible guide on our own journey of discovery of
who we are and what our personal destiny means in this
great cosmic context.

If galaxies were frozen peas there would be enough of them
to fill the Albert Hall.
Bill Bryson

We belong to a web of creation in which nothing, absolutely nothing, is inconsequential. The hairs of your head, a baby's sneeze, the gravitational pull of an electron at the far edge of the Milky Way – none of these things is negligible. Not one of them can be subtracted from creation, or even rounded off, without changing the whole gorgeous geometry of the universe... Every one of us will change the world, whether we mean to or not.
Barbara Brown Taylor[21]

Each of us will change the world. Our hearts are programmed for it and we will find no contentment until we discover, and live true to, our eternal destiny, at one within ourselves, and at one within the entire web of being that is life.

In the rest of this book, we explore some of the ways in which this great quest has proceeded, and continues to emerge, until the Dream is fully dreamed.

**Life is something endlessly in the process
of becoming something else.**
Richard Holloway

Natural Wisdom

I met a tree today. I could have walked straight past her and
she wouldn't have interrupted my busy schedule. But I'm
very glad I stopped to talk... or rather to listen. Because the
tree had so much to tell me of her own wisdom...

She told me how much the earth had shown her through
her two hundred years on our planet, rooted here, in the
place where I live myself.

She spoke softly of the cycles of life that play themselves
out in her roots and boughs; how it is sometimes so cold,
sometimes wet, and sometimes the sun shines. All come
from God, she says, and all seasons have their reasons. She
blossoms and fruits in the summer, and sleeps in winter,
whether the sky is blue or grey.

She told me how hard it is to let go of her beautiful
leaves when the November winds blow through her
branches, but how, if she held on to them too tightly, there
would be no energy left to keep her roots alive. She told me
of the joy of each spring awakening, just when she thinks
there will be no more awakening, and how this has taught

If a bacterium observed and examined a human nail,
it would pronounce it inorganic matter;

her to trust, and to hang on to life through the dark sleep of winter.

She whispered to me with pride of how she had begun her life as a tiny acorn that had rotted in the ground until the first beginnings of everything she would become had poked through the cold earth, and how every branch of her body now bears hundreds of acorns, and how each one may become not just another oak, but the parent of a whole forest of oaks, and how strange it is that one has to die in order to live.

She shared with me the wisdom her experience has grown in her:

how it is sometimes better to bend than to break;

how it is necessary to let the blossoms fall, to make way for the fruit, and to let the fruit fall to nourish the creatures of the forest, and to strengthen her own roots;

how the leaves she grieves to lose become the blanket of her winter sleep, sheltering her dream until the sun returns;

how she quivers with joy when the children play among her boughs, and how she shudders with dread when the lightning strikes, and how both are part of life, and ask for our consent;

how the fresh leaves at the tips of her branches have no idea of the vast structure of life, of boughs and trunk and roots that hold them in being and bring them to their awakening, but how they awaken anyway, without needing to know why and how;

and how good it is to be, and to grow, and to trust.

---

and thus we, with reference to the globe, examine its crust and pronounce it inorganic. This is incorrect.
Leo Tolstoy

Wisdom holds the world in being

Perhaps the tree is wiser in her way than we can be, for the
natural world has its own deep logic, and all its wisdom is
directed towards the continuance of life. This deep natural
wisdom runs through every aspect of the natural world,
guiding and animating everything, from the starry expanses
of the cosmos, down to the intricate life of a single atom of
our own bodies.

Paul Davies expresses his sense of wonder at this reality:

*We've emerged from nature. We belong here in the universe
as part of the natural order... I think the existence of not
just conscious minds, but of beings who can also make sense
of the world, is a fact of staggering importance... We are
not only animated stardust. We're stardust capable of
understanding how the stars came to exist in the first place.*
Paul Davies[1]

Rabbi David Nelson reminds us of the miracle of self-
organization that shapes each manifestation of the infinite
variety of nature into what it is destined to become,
however tiny, however vast:

*The awe inspired by a starry night is no different from
that inspired by a stormy sea, or a single whale leaping
from the waves, or, for that matter, by a sleeping child or
the tightly fisted hand of a newborn infant. Indeed, the
structure of a DNA strand and that of a galaxy both seem*

**Stir the water and you get waves. Stir the gene pool
and you get eyes, kidneys, spinal cords and brains.**
Barbara Brown Taylor

to indicate the presence of a sophisticated, structuring force, an agency of order in the universe. So just as the coastline of Britain 'grows' infinitely large as we measure it in smaller and smaller increments, I am awed by the way the 'measurements' of God grow without limit as we examine them on ever smaller scales.
Rabbi David W. Nelson[2]

Barbara Brown Taylor expresses this sense of wonder with a poet's voice, noticing how the superabundance of Life has its origin in the dust cast forth upon space by the supernova explosions of ancient stars in their death-throes. From such a dust-cloud, a deep, creating wisdom, constantly seeking to bring more and more life into being, organizes almost nothing into everything imaginable, through what she calls 'the dynamics of self-organization':

Stir the water and you get waves. Stir the gene pool and you get eyes, kidneys, spinal cords and brains. Stir it again and the details may change, but the patterns will remain familiar, thanks to the dynamics of self-organization.

Dust is all God has ever needed to make life: the quantum dust from which the stars arose, the stardust by which the primal elements were sown, the earth dust from which the rocks were made, and the rock dust on which the first creatures grew.
Barbara Brown Taylor[3]

Spend the afternoon. You can't take it with you.
Annie Dillard

The Genesis writer expresses the same truth:

Yahweh God shaped man from the soil of the ground and blew the breath of life into his nostrils, and man became a living being.
Genesis 2:7

What the Genesis writer describes as 'the breath of life', we might today perhaps describe in terms of the energy of creation, while remaining no more able to name and define the source of that all-pervading life force than our early forebears. We know only that any definitions will fall far short of the truth. And yet we see the evidence of nature's 'knowing' in every aspect of creation.

Another poet-voice, that of Michael Mayne, rejoices in God's obvious love for God's creation, and in the profound mystery that shapes matter into a created world capable of embodying the very spirit of its creator:

'God likes matter', it has been said, 'he invented it'. Matter: rock, water, wood, grass, birds, corn, grapes, cells. Not only does God like it but he clothes himself in it. It is one of his languages.

Ours is a world that is unimaginably more than the ordered mass of atoms and molecules obeying the rules of their separate fields. For it is a world in which matter is capable of being the bearer of spirit.

Listen to and respect those who cannot bring themselves

There are two hundred and twenty-eight separate and distinct muscles in the head of an ordinary caterpillar.
Annie Dillard

to believe in God, especially those who cannot reconcile the pain they feel or the hurt they have been done, with a God whose nature is love. But never give any credence to those who say they believe, yet would remove God from his world.

Michael Mayne[4]

This same deep wisdom, or 'knowing', reveals itself in the inner workings of the cells that constitute our own bodies. It forms and shapes us from first conception:

The same speck of DNA deposited in the womb knows how to perform millions of actions that will not be needed for years or even decades to come. Our genes know how to fuse an infant's loosely joined skull bones and at the same time how to compensate for lost calcium in a seventy-year-old femur. It has been estimated that six trillion chemical reactions take place in the body every second. The same speck of DNA controls them all, rarely mistiming a single one.

Deepak Chopra[5]

And it continues to hold us in being for as long as we live:

…amid the phenomenal complexity of biology, there exists an underlying simplicity so eloquent that it is expressed in a single molecule. A single cell at fertilization contained within

---

**Nature is reasserting herself as a subtle web
of spirit and connectedness.**
Robert Fripp

it all the potential that you were ever physically to become. And every cell within your body retains that wisdom.

Every second of every minute of every day, your body and every body is organizing in the order of 150 thousand thousand thousand thousand thousand thousand thousand amino acids into carefully constructed chains of proteins. Every second; every minute; every day. The fabric from which we and all life are built is being continually rewoven at a most astoundingly rapid rate.

The biological system of information storage is phenomenally dense. If all the information in all the libraries in all languages were transcribed into the language of DNA, it could be recorded within a volume equivalent to 1 percent of the head of a pin.

Gerald Schroeder[6]

Connecting to nature's wisdom

To access this deep underlying wisdom in all things doesn't require some superhuman intellect. While the scientists can astound us with their revelations of how nature works, we are not required to understand it but to respond to it, to relate to it, and to fulfil our place within it, simply by becoming who we truly are. In our modern world, the practice of meditation invites us to enter into a deeper reality, which we do not control, but may contemplate, and as we contemplate it, we begin to intuit our oneness with it and our own role within it. The practice of meditation is not bounded by any one

---

The practice of looking deeply reveals to us that one thing is made up of all other things.

spiritual tradition, but is a process that all may enter into, whether they consider themselves to be 'religious' or not.

It is said that when Mount Everest was climbed for the first time in 1953, Edmund Hilary planted a flag on the summit, as any Western 'conqueror' would have done, while his companion, Sherpa Tensing, knelt down in the snow and begged the mountain's forgiveness for disturbing its peace. This is the difference between conquering nature and responding to it, between dominating it and relating to it. Tensing's response flowed from a deep and contemplative relationship to the world around him.

The mystic, Thich Nhat Hanh, has helped very many present-day pilgrims to draw from this deep well of the heart:

> Imagine that we are a wave on the ocean, and surrounding us are many, many waves. If the wave looks deeply within herself, she will realize that her being there depends on the presence of all the other waves. Her coming up, her going down, and her being big or small depend entirely on how the other waves are. Looking into yourself, you touch the whole, you touch everything – you are conditioned by what is there around you...
>
> But there is another level of relationship, and that is the relationship between the wave and the water. The wave is aware that she is made of the other waves, and at the same time she realizes that she is made of water too. It is very important for her to touch the water, the foundation of her

---

One thing contains the whole cosmos.
Thich Nhat Hanh

being. She realizes that the other waves are also made of water…

The practice of looking deeply reveals to us that one thing is made up of all other things. One thing contains the whole cosmos.

The wave may be aware that it is made of water. But the wave may be so bound to the suffering and the difficulty she is having with other waves that she is not able to realize that she is in an intimate relationship with water, and water is also the ground of all the other waves.
Thich Nhat Hanh[7]

Far from being just a beautiful image or a gateway into prayer, this reflection goes to the heart of what it means to be both who we are as individuals, and at the same time in full and right relationship with the ground of all our being, and hence, with each other.

Brian Swimme says something very similar about the contemplation of our own solar system. It isn't, he tells us, about understanding its workings with our minds, but, more importantly, about entering into the living reality of it with our hearts and our entire consciousness:

To fully understand, one has to sit down and wait for the universe to enter.

But if you do so, you will become one of a very small number of humans who actually live in the solar system. Most humans live not on the Earth that rotates and revolves

---

To fully understand, one has to sit down and wait for the universe to enter.
Brian Swimme

about the Sun. We live rather in a fantasy that regards the Earth as a fixed place, where the ground is always stationary; that regards the planet as somehow resting on a great slab of cement. But to contemplate the solar system until you feel the great Earth turning away from the Sun and until you feel this immense planet being swung around its massive cosmic partner is to touch an ocean of wonder as you take a first step into inhabiting the actual universe and solar system and Earth.

Brian Swimme[8]

To connect, in our hearts, to this presence of God in God's creation, is to share something of Wordsworth's intuition in his poem 'Lines composed a few miles above Tintern Abbey, 1798':

> *And I have felt*
> *A presence that disturbs me with the joy*
> *Of elevated thoughts; a sense sublime*
> *Of something far more deeply interfused,*
> *Whose dwelling is the light of setting suns,*
> *And the round ocean and the living air,*
> *And the blue sky, and in the mind of man;*
> *A motion and a spirit, that impels*
> *All thinking things, all objects of all thought,*
> *And rolls through all things.*

> **William Wordsworth[9]**

We are not only animated stardust. We're stardust capable of understanding how the stars came to exist in the first place.
Paul Davies

In prose, and two centuries later, Keith Ward re-echoes this sense of a presence invisible, interwoven through all that is:

The authentic religious sense is to discern infinity and eternity in the bounded and transient, to see in all particular forms of beauty a Beauty which is unlimited in perfection and everlasting in value. The sense of an interfused presence, living in the light and air and sky, and in the mind of man: the sense of such a presence, splitting, like light, into a thousand glittering shafts of individuality, each taking on the character of its own environment: the sense of a world filled with presences sublime and interfused, many and yet one, beautiful and harsh, wine-dark and rose-fingered: that is the sense of the gods, who excite human reverence and awe, dread and delight.
Keith Ward[10]

To enter into the mystery of things is an invitation that nature presents us with over and over again, if we 'have time to stand and stare'. The presence of the wisdom of God in creation calls to the spirit within us, answers a longing we didn't even realize we had:

The texture of the world, its filigree and scrollwork, means that there is the possibility for beauty here, a beauty inexhaustible in its complexity, which opens to my knock,

---

Evolution is not in itself the process of change, but rather the process by which

which answers in me a call I do not remember calling, and
which trains me to the wild and extravagant nature of the
spirit I seek.
Annie Dillard[11]

It is no great distance from this realization to the
dawning awareness that God is in all and all is in God, and
that each of us is held in the All. Joseph Mary Plunkett
finds this omnipresence in all of creation:

> *I see his blood upon the rose*
> *And in the stars the glory of his eyes,*
> *His body gleams amid eternal snows,*
> *His tears fall from the skies.*
>
> *I see his face in every flower;*
> *The thunder and the singing of the birds*
> *Are but his voice – and carven by his power*
> *Rocks are his written words.*
> *All pathways by his feet are worn,*
> *His strong heart stirs the ever-beating sea.*
> *His crown of thorns is twined with every thorn,*
> *His cross is every tree.*
> **Joseph Mary Plunkett**[12]

And this Irish voice is echoed by a Filipino song of
praise. Each of them expresses the universal wisdom
of God as revealed in a very specific and particular part

---

life as a whole seeks continuity
through the vicissitudes of change.
Robert Fripp

of God's creation. It is a response that has a thousand other echoes from every corner of the world.

> *I am the sunrise that brightens up the sky in the early morning.*
> *I am the rays of the sun that give radiance to every creature*
> *during the sunrise at Manila Bay.*
> *I am the fire that kindles the stars, and the stars in your eyes.*
> *I am the white sand kissed by the bubbling waves of the blue seas.*
> *I am the fresh smell of the rice fields.*
> *I am the trunk of a talisay tree standing amidst the polluted and*
> *overpopulated areas.*
> *I am the sturdy bamboo that sways unbroken by strong winds.*
> *I am the sweat of an oppressed people.*
> *I am the smile on the lips of a fallen comrade.*
> *I am the tears of a mother in pain.*
> *I am the colour of the rainbow that gives hope.*
> *I am the forlorn trees resisting extinction.*
> *I am what I am – the Holy god of the universe who is of all,*
> *in all, under all, over all, all.*
> **Filipino reflection**[13]

A universe of patterns and interrelationships

Once we allow ourselves to be a part of the natural world, rather than imagining ourselves to be its conquerors, we begin to see the pervasive patterns that govern the life of all things. We discover, for example, that our home planet is far from being an inert lump of rock, but is in fact a finely-

---

Looking at the Earth from afar you realize it is too small for conflict and just big enough for cooperation.
Yuri Gagarin (the first person in space)

tuned living organism with the power of self-regulation.

On the return trip home, gazing through 240,000 miles of space towards the stars and the planet from which I had come, I suddenly experienced the universe as intelligent, loving and harmonious. My view of the planet was a glimpse of divinity.
Edgar Mitchell (looking down on Earth from space)

The climate and the chemical properties of the Earth now and throughout its history seem always to have been optimal for life. For this to have happened by chance is as unlikely as to survive unscathed a drive blindfold through rush-hour traffic.
James Lovelock[14]

Not only is the earth a living organism, but it supports an abundance of life forms which themselves can only exist in relationship and interconnection with each other. Relationship – which means right relationship – is the only basis from which life can flourish. When we sever or damage relationship we cut ourselves off from the very life that is in us.

Especially in the realm of living beings there is an absolute inter-dependency. No living being nourishes itself. There exists a sequence of dissolution and renewal, a death–life sequence that has continued in Earth for some billions of years. This capacity for self-renewal through seeds that bond

---

Everything that is in the heavens, on the earth, and under the earth is penetrated with connectedness, penetrated with relatedness.
Hildegard of Bingen

*one generation of life to a successor generation is especially
precious to the animal world, which feeds on the excess of
plant life produced each year. Every animal form depends
ultimately on plant forms that alone can transform the
energy of the sun and the minerals of Earth into the living
substance needed for life nourishment of the entire animal
world, including the human community.*
Thomas Berry[15]

Yet to be in right relationship, knowing ourselves to be
one with the whole, held by it, not in control of it, is to
have access to the power of life to an extraordinary degree,
whether we are caterpillars or kings, or the magnificent
albatross encountered by Philip Yancey off the coast of New
Zealand, whose flight is powered by a living, breathing,
high-tech system that puts our lumbering jetliners seriously
in the shade:

*Between whale sightings the guide, a Maori biologist,
described other sea life. When a royal albatross soared by, he
rhapsodised about these 'kings of the air'. Their wings,
spanning 11 feet (3.3 metres) are so well-designed that an
albatross can cover 600 miles with less flapping of its wings
than a sparrow needs to cross a street. An albatross can sleep
on the wing, flying on autopilot thanks to a small windspeed
recorder in its bill that sends data to the brain, allowing it to
make wing adjustments as the wind shifts. Also, an albatross
has a built-in desalination factory. When it scoops up a*

**Within our bodies are something like 50 trillion different
cells, all interrelating to keep us alive.**
Michael Mayne

mouthful of ocean, a series of tubes and membranes in the
bill processes the water and extrudes excess salt.
Philip Yancey[16]

If this is how God equips the birds of the air, what has God given to us, and are we really in touch with its amazing power for life?

The horseshoe crab Limulus breeds once a year, precisely at
the full moon nearest to midsummer day. It is then that the
highest tide falls near the longest day of the year. Limulus's
innate sense of several circadian rhythms is such that, one
month later, when the next full moon brings the next highest
tide, young horseshoe crabs emerge from the sand and float
back to sea in the receding water...
Robert Fripp[17]

If this is how God, through the wisdom of nature, equips a little crab to survive and reproduce itself, by obeying its deep inner rhythms, what are we missing in our lives, when we disregard the rhythms of our bodies, minds and hearts? Shortly after the catastrophic Asian tsunami that claimed so many lives on 26 December 2004, I met a lady from Sri Lanka. She told me how, days before the tsunami struck, all the elephants had disappeared from the coastal regions, and I am told that the ants and many other wild creatures in Thailand migrated in a similar manner. Perhaps the ants and the elephants have more

---

At birth there was already enough information capacity in every single cell in my body to fill some dozen copies of the Encyclopaedia Britannica.
Michael Mayne

intelligence in the soles of their feet than we have in all our state-of-the-art technology.

> *Can you not buy five sparrows for two pennies? And yet not one is forgotten in God's sight. Why, every hair on your head has been counted. There is no need to be afraid; you are worth more than many sparrows.*
> Luke 12:6–7

If we really believed this, what difference would it make to the way we see ourselves – and the ways we see each other?

Diairmuid Ó'Murchú challenges us to 'think big' when we reflect on God and God's creation, and to enter into the mystery that pre-dates all our religions and will still be growing and unfolding itself long after formal religion has passed into history.

> *The wisdom story is bigger than Christianity and indeed exceeds in grandeur and elegance all the insights of the great religions… The wise and holy God was at work for billions of years before religious consciousness began to develop. And that same creative wisdom will continue to beget radically new possibilities, for ever defying and challenging the outstanding theories and inventions of the human mind…*
>
> *We belong beautifully to the earth. It is the alive, maternal organism that brought us into being, sustains us*

Split a piece of wood; I am there. Lift a piece of stone, and you will find me there.
from the Gnostic Gospel of St Thomas

throughout life, and receives us back into the fertile earth
when our lives have run their course. Death is not the
consequence of sin in a sinful world. Death is both a
natural and a supernatural dimension of life recycling its
resources, not in a mindless merry-go-round that never goes
anywhere, but in a process resembling a spiral, always
moving to realms of greater depth as evolution begets new
possibilities from the death and transformation of old forms.
Diairmuid Ó'Murchú[18]

An every-moment miracle

To grow in awareness of the wisdom that holds the natural
world in being is to become day by day more conscious of
the ever-recurring miracles along the way. We tend to look
for the miraculous in a supernatural context, and yet the
great Miracle Worker himself urged us to find God in the
everyday miracles in the world we live and work in. Those
with eyes to see have discovered the truth of his guiding
ever since. In the words of Wendell Berry:

The miraculous is not extraordinary but the common mode
of existence. It is our daily bread. Whoever really has
considered the lilies of the field or the birds of the air and
pondered the improbability of their existence in this warm
world within the cold and empty stellar distances will hardly
baulk at the turning of water into wine – which was, after
all, a very small miracle. We forget the greater and still

What if some genius were to do with 'common life' what Einstein
did with matter? Finding its energies, uncovering its radiance.
Saul Bellow

*continuing miracle by which water (with soil and sunlight)
is turned into grapes.*

And no less an authority than Augustine of Hippo points
out the same truth:

*We take for granted the slow miracle of nature whereby a
vineyard is irrigated and the water eventually becomes wine.
It is only when Christ turns water instantly to wine that we
are so utterly astonished.*
Augustine of Hippo[19]

And if we can, just for even a fleeting moment, become
aware of the miracle of our own living being, we will never
be quite the same again, either in our self or in our sense of
being connected to all life:

*I looked at my hands and imagined how dead hands look.
I felt my face, to get some idea of the form of the dead skull
which was in me. I tried to imagine myself as a cold and
lifeless corpse. But as I touched my body, I felt how warm it
was. My heart beat regularly. My breath went in and out.
My eyes saw the starry sky. My ears heard the lapping of
the lake. My nose smelt the smell of sand and salt water.
I saw, heard, smelt. I lived, breathed and felt. Wasn't it a
miracle that dust and earth could live, think and feel, doubt
and despair? Think how many processes in my body had to
take place regularly for me to be able to experience this*

**Angel nor saint have I seen,
But I have heard the roar of the western sea,**

moment without bodily pain! And if it was only a transitory moment – was it any the less worthwhile for that?…

I felt that my life was part of the life that was given. In me lived on something of all men and women, the happy and the unhappy… Wasn't there deep within me the intimation of a life which could not attain fulfilment by being against others but only by being alongside them? In which everyone, the fortunate and the unfortunate, were bound together as closely as the members of a body.

Gerd Thiessen[20]

We respond best to the miracle of life when we refrain from interfering with it for our own ends, even though our intentions may be good, and when we let go of our self-centred need to control things. There is a sad story of a schoolboy who tried, with the highest motives, to speed up the emergence of a butterfly, with fatal consequences:

I remember one morning when I discovered a cocoon in the bark of a tree, just as the butterfly was making a hole in its case and preparing to come out. I waited a while, but it was too long appearing and I was impatient. I bent over it and breathed on it to warm it. I warmed it as quickly as I could and the miracle began to happen before my eyes, faster than life. The case opened, the butterfly started slowly crawling out and I shall never forget my horror when I saw how its wings were folded back and crumpled. The wretched butterfly tried with its whole trembling body to unfold them.

And the isle of my heart is in the midst of it.
Attributed to St Columba

Bending over it, I tried to help it with my breath. In vain. It needed to be hatched out patiently and the unfolding of the wings should be a gradual process in the sun. Now it was too late. My breath had forced the butterfly to appear, all crumpled before its time. It struggled desperately, and a few seconds later, died in the palm of my hand.

That little body is, I do believe, the greatest weight I have on my conscience. For I realize today that it is a mortal sin to violate the great laws of nature. We should not be impatient, but we should confidently obey the eternal rhythm.
Nikos Kazantzakis[21]

A similar disastrous pattern of interference can be seen over and over again, as we try to guide our children's learning with a too-heavy hand – it is so much easier to do things for them than to allow them to develop their own skills, by making their own mistakes. To stand back and watch nature get on with her great enterprise demands a high degree of humility and a hefty portion of patience – neither of which are in plentiful supply among the human race. It also challenges us to do some discerning about how far we can, and should, go in cooperating with nature's venture (for example, by cultivating our gardens and caring for other living creatures) and when we need to tread softly and reverently, allowing God to be God.

To know how little we really know is the beginning of wisdom:

**A bird does not sing because it has an answer;
it sings because it has a song.**
Chinese proverb

I am formed of the matter of the universe and I am linked through it to the remotest stars in time and space. My body has passed through all the stages of evolution through which matter has passed over millions of years. I have been present when matter was first formed into atoms and molecules, when the living cell appeared. I have passed through every stage from protoplasm to fish and animal and man. If I could know myself, I would know matter and life, animal and man, since all are contained within me. In all this long evolution my mind has been developing with my body. There was a mind latent in matter, latent in the living cell, which has gradually emerged into consciousness. My mind has recapitulated every stage of human consciousness from the most primitive state of awareness to the reflective consciousness I enjoy now. But most of this remains buried in my unconscious. How little of myself do I really know. My conscious knowledge is only the tip of an iceberg which reaches down to the depths of the abyss from which my existence first emerged.

Bede Griffiths[22]

Antoine de Saint-Exupéry, encapsulates all of this wisdom in the words of his little prince contemplating the solitary rose he has grown:

'The men where you live,' said the little prince, 'raise five thousand roses in the same garden – and they do not find in it what they are looking for.'
'They do not find it,' I replied.

**Let me learn the lessons you have hidden
in every leaf and rock.**
Native American prayer

*'And yet what they are looking for could be found in a
single rose, or in a little water.'*
   'Yes, that is true,' I said.
   And the little prince added:
   'But the eyes are blind. One must look with the heart...'
Antoine de Saint-Exupéry[23]

Truly, to see the wisdom of God we must look with the
heart, and the one who looks with the heart shall see more
than the mind could possibly imagine.

The world is charged with the grandeur of God.
It will flame out, like shining from shook foil.
Gerard Manley Hopkins

Indigenous Wisdom

Whether we are scientists or mystics, whether we deal in reason or in dreams, we are human beings, and what human beings do, above all, is to search for meaning in the vast mystery around us. There are those who would say that this restless quest is simply an antidote to the sure knowledge that after a few short decades each of us will die. But there would be many who would beg to differ, and would argue that the very fact that humankind is perpetually on a quest for wisdom and meaning is itself a sure pointer to the presence of a Wisdom that is eternally holding us in being, and unfolding its multilayered meaning to our finite hearts.

Conceivably for as long as three hundred thousand years, humans have huddled together in the night to ponder and to celebrate the mysteries of the universe in order to find their way through the Great World they inhabit. No matter what continent humans lived on, no matter what culture, no matter what era, the work of cosmology took place every

---

**Man did not weave the web of life; he is merely a strand in it.
Whatever he does to the web he does to himself.**
Chief Seathl

year and every month and even every day – around the fire
of the African plains, in the caves of the Eurasian forests,
under the brilliant night sky of the Australian land mass, in
the long houses of North America. There the people told the
sacred stories of how the world came to be, of what the
human brings into the universe, and of what it takes to live
a noble life within the Great Holy that is the universe.
Brian Swimme[1]

Walking the earth with reverence

When our ancient forebears were not huddled round the
campfire to ponder the great mysteries, they were walking
with light and sensitive steps on the earth that sustained
their life. This is a 'message from forever' attributed to Bee
Lake, an Australian Aboriginal mystic:

Forever Oneness,
Who sings to us in silence,
Who teaches us through each other,
Guide my steps with strength and wisdom.
May I see the lessons as I walk,
Honour the purpose of all things.
Help me touch with respect,
Always speak from behind my eyes.
Let me observe, not judge.
May I cause no harm, and leave
Music and beauty after my visit.

Only after the last tree has been cut down.
Only after the last river has been poisoned.

When I return to forever,
May the circle be closed and
The spiral broader.
Marlo Morgan[2]

To hear the song in the silence, to learn from each other and all creatures, to honour the purpose of everything that is 'other', to touch all creation with respect, to see it with an inner vision, to leave nothing behind us except the eternal effects of what is good and true and beautiful in our living, this is what the quest asks of us. To walk the earth with this degree of reverence, this sharpness of observation and gentleness of response, is an ideal that finds expression in the Aboriginal tradition of 'walkabout', which demands a total trust in creation and its creator:

Australian Aborigines do an exercise to express trust in their Creator that can put the rest of us to shame. They leave the village for months for a 'walkabout' in the wilderness with absolutely no provisions to make the journey safe or easy. They simply trust that as they walk barefoot through the wilderness their needs for food, water and shelter will be met. And they are! One observer declared that they must perform some sort of magic, because when they are hungry, food miraculously appears. I believe it is because these Aborigines simply trust Creation.

Fran Dancing Feather and Rita Robinson[3]

Only after the last fish has been caught.
Only then will you find that money cannot be eaten.
Cree Indian prophecy

For the Celts too, life was a quest in search of wisdom and eternal meaning. The greatest challenge and the greatest adventure was to set foot in the coracle and sail the seas, surrendering the safety of dry land, trusting only in God for guidance in a wild, uncharted world. We may not literally step into a coracle today, and our planet has been largely charted and tamed, and yet in our lived experience there will always be calls to leave the comfort zone and venture where, perhaps, we would rather not go, and yet where we will grow in wisdom if we dare to take the risk.

> *An insatiable questing was part of the Celtic spirit, a longing to see what lay over the horizon, for living close to the sea affects the senses... But it was not simply the physical presence of the sea. The sea is a place of liminality, a boundary, a frontier, between two places and if the search is for the meaning of life what better place in which to site it? So the sea also becomes a place of revelation, a source of wisdom, a medium through which messages come from the 'other-world'.*
> **Esther de Waal**[4]

To be on a quest for what always lies beyond us seems to be a fundamental characteristic of what it means to be human. It takes us to the boundary between the known and unknown, the visible and invisible, a liminal place, where transformations happen and we are invited to transcend whatever is limiting our present understanding and experience.

There are no accidents, only spiritual connections from which we have not distanced ourselves far enough to see.
Marlo Morgan

The quest can lead to the vision, and the vision can lead to new dimensions of wisdom which can then be communicated to the whole community for the healing and enrichment of all creation:

> *Visions are gifts that provide answers to questions posed in prayer. The main religions of the world, all of which contain sacred texts or scriptures, were written as groups of stories or directions given to their followers by individuals who had experienced the gift of sacred knowledge within their physical lives.*
>
> *Many practised something akin to a vision quest in order to acquire the knowledge of which they wrote. Nearly all of the stories illustrate how the destructive nature of humankind can be turned around. The revelations received by the prophet or visionary showed men and women how to turn poison into medicine.*
>
> **Fran Dancing Feather and Rita Robinson**[5]

The web of life

A theme that permeates every expression of indigenous wisdom is that of the supreme importance of a sense of the wholeness and oneness of all creation, and the fact that every creature is intimately interconnected and interrelated with every other. It follows that everything any of us does affects all of us. This gives us a powerful sense of belonging, but it also evokes an awareness of responsibility. The fossil

---

Turning poison into medicine is the great act of the supernatural in our lives.
Fran Dancing Feather and Rita Robinson

evidence reveals that our early ancestors demonstrated this sense of co-responsibility. They cared for the very young and the very old, tended the sick and injured, often with a more searching knowledge of the healing properties of the plants and trees around them than we have ourselves, and they buried the dead. They understood that to abuse and exploit the earth was to damage themselves, and they acted accordingly. This profound wisdom comes down to us still, through their living traditions, with an urgency that we ignore at our peril:

> *Whatever befalls the earth, befalls the sons of the earth.*
> *If men spit upon the ground, they spit upon themselves.*
> *This we know. The earth does not belong to man; man belongs*
> *To the earth. This we know. All things are connected like*
> *The blood which unites one family. All things are connected.*
> *Whatever befalls the earth befalls the sons of the earth.*
> *Man did not weave the web of life; he is merely a strand in it.*
> *Whatever he does to the web he does to himself.*
> **Chief Seathl**[6]

The intimacy of the experience of oneness with all creation is often expressed by thinking of the ancestors as wise 'grandparents' who now, reunited with eternity, could guide those still on the earthly quest with the benefit of the accumulated wisdom of all times and people. Far from being an idolatrous 'ancestor-worship', this is a way of saying 'We are more than the sum of our own small world

---

Now he understood Aboriginal art. It wasn't meant to be hung on a wall. It was meant to be viewed from above.

of personal experience and wisdom; we must draw on all that has gone before, for it flows down to us from the Creator.' In this prayer of the Ojibway people of Canada, God himself is addressed as 'Grandfather'.

Grandfather,
Look at our brokenness.
We know that in all creation
Only the human family
Has strayed from the Sacred Way.
We know that we are the ones
Who are divided
And we are the ones
Who must come back together
To walk in the Sacred way.
Grandfather,
Sacred One,
Teach us love, compassion and honour
That we may heal the earth
And heal each other.
Ojibway prayer[7]

When we understand the essential unity of all that is, we discover the possibility of 'peace' – the kind of peace that in Hebrew is called 'Shalom', which is infinitely more than the absence of strife; it is the wholeness of the web of life itself and of every creature in it, held in the wholeness of the one God.

It was drawn as a scene would be seen from the sky,
the eye of Oneness looking upon creation.
Marlo Morgan

*Peace comes within the souls of men when they realise their
relationship, their oneness, with the universe and all its
powers, and when they realise that at the centre of the
Universe dwells Wakan-Tanka [the Great Spirit], and that
this centre is really everywhere, it is within each of us.*
Matthew Fox[8]

Matthew Fox goes on to quote from the 'Zulu Personal
Declaration' composed in South Africa in 1825:

I;
I am;
I am alive;
I am conscious and aware;
I am unique;

I am who I say I am; I am the value UQOBO [essence]
*I forever evolve inwardly and outwardly in response to the
challenge of my nature;*
I am the face of humanity;
The face of humanity is my face.

And from the other side of the world, the same theme re-
echoes, reminding us that the invisible web of relationship
in which we are all held is as vital to us collectively, as our
blood circulatory system is to us individually. To be aware
of this web of relationship, to heed its call, to respect its
demands and to participate in its wisdom, this is holiness:

**According to Native American wisdom, the only way that evil
can penetrate the human heart is through the door of fear.**
Matthew Fox

Central to White Buffalo Woman's message, to all native spirituality, is the understanding that the Great Spirit lives in all things, enlivens all forms, and gives energy to all things in all realms of creation – including Earthly life…

Ancient teachings call us to turn primary attention to the Sacred Web of Life, of which we are a part and with which we are so obviously entangled. This quality of attention – paying attention to the whole – is called among my people 'holiness'.
Brooke Medicine Eagle[9]

Such a sense of oneness kindles a very different attitude towards the sanctity of others, and their right to be who they are, for, as David Monongye reminds us, we are all flowers in the same garden:

We are all flowers in the Great Spirit's garden. We share a common root, and the root is Mother Earth. The garden is beautiful because it has different colours in it, and those colours represent different traditions and cultural backgrounds.
Grandfather David Monongye[10]

During a visit to the central deserts of Australia I was amazed at the peaceable attitude of the Aboriginal people, as I began to learn something of their history and the relative lack of resistance they had shown to the European colonists who moved into their ancestral lands. I mentioned this to an Aboriginal companion. He seemed surprised at my question, and his reply left me speechless.

Head talk is a product of society. Heart talk is from Forever.
Marlo Morgan

'The land doesn't belong to us,' he said, 'we belong to the land.'

For him and his people it was a logical progression from this point of view to allow that anyone else who might choose to settle these lands likewise belongs to the land. The tragedy of indigenous peoples, of course, is that the European colonists have never shared their understanding of humankind's place in the great web of life. Marlo Morgan picks up something of this spirit of tolerance:

You acknowledge all people as forever souls, acknowledge all people as being on their journey through the school of human experience, and acknowledge all souls as possessing the gift of free will and freedom of choice given by the Creator. In other words, people different from yourself are not wrong. They are just making different spiritual choices...

All people are Forever spirits, even the blue-eyed Europeans who call this earth Australia and think they own it. For all souls, the same truths apply. They don't have to agree, but truth is truth, spirit law is law, and so, in the end, all people will wake up and know...

What our people have been saying all this time is that what makes up a cloud is also what makes up you. You are part sun, moon, star, water, fire, dingo. Do you understand what I mean? It is all one.

Marlo Morgan[11]

The way in which we deal with difficult people is the acid test of who we are and how we use the tools of our spiritual path.
Fran Dancing Feather and Rita Robinson

Reaping from the past, planting for the future

Wisdom isn't an individualistic attainment, nor is it a commodity that manifests itself in a chosen few. It isn't 'the icing on the cake' that we can indulge in when we have enough bread to eat, nor does any individual, or nation or religious tradition own a monopoly on it.

It is a flow of profound understanding that sees into the nature of life. It is a cumulative gift that we receive from those who lived before us and must be passed on to those who follow after, with the addition of whatever wisdom the experience of our own generation reveals.

It is not surprising, therefore, that indigenous spiritualities include a profound reverence for the 'elders'. To be old in an indigenous community is to be revered as one who has lived long, experienced much, and therefore, potentially, has a great deal of wisdom to impart.

We feel pride when we share the wisdom left to us by our elders. Once we know something about our people and their places of origin we can begin to practise the native concept of the 'giveaway', the most profound act of sharing our physical, mental, and spiritual elements with others. This act of generosity, which can also include material possessions (such as food, crafts and sacred objects), draws people from other cultures to us, and we see them begin to share a part of themselves. This gesture adds to the wisdom from which we draw as we begin the path of self-discovery that helps us define our quest in this life...

You are accountable for your body. It is a gift borrowed from the elements that your consciousness helped form and gave life to.
Marlo Morgan

It is good medicine to surround ourselves with people whom we consider to be more highly evolved or more enlightened than we are. We can interact with them ourselves, or watch and listen to them relate to one another in gatherings…

The secrets of the heart are those wonderful gifts we are born with that live in our DNA, and are available to us whenever we need them. Everything we ever want to know about the wisdom of the ancients is already in our hearts. We are truly more spiritual than physical, and it is our quest to come into union with this internal wisdom.

Fran Dancing Feather and Rita Robinson[12]

I remember a personal 'elder' in my life who first introduced me to the Indian notion of the four sacred stages of life, and in particular to the stage of the elder who withdraws to the forest to consolidate a life's wisdom before passing on to transcendence after death. The man who taught me this was just such a person himself, who had gathered his life's wisdom together, shared it with many others, in his relationships, his teaching and his writings, and was now preparing for the final stage of his earthly journey. As he lay dying, he had reminders all around him of his journey, and those special people who had shaped and formed him, and he delighted in telling me something of his encounters with these people. Then, as death came closer, he quite consciously let them go, one by one, giving thanks for everything, until, on a

---

We do not inherit the Earth from our Ancestors,
we borrow it from our Children.
Native American proverb

beautiful May morning, he relinquished his own hold on this life, and returned to the Eternal Now. I cherish his memory. He showed me what an 'elder' is, but also left me wondering how much we have lost in a society that so easily derides old age, and locks it away out of sight, and out of mind.

One of the legacies of my 'elder' friend was an appreciation of the work of Bede Griffiths, a man he greatly admired.

In ancient Indian society there were four ashramas, or stages of life. The first was that of the brahmachari, the student or 'seeker of God', who has to acquire the knowledge necessary both for life in this world and for that which is to come. The next stage is that of the householder, who raises a family and builds up the city and the State. But this is followed by that of the vanaprastha and the sannyasi, retirement to the forest and finally renunciation of the world to prepare for 'liberation'. This is the basic pattern of human society, as was realized in one way or another in all the ancient world. The modern world has lost this orientation towards a transcendent state. It has stopped at the second stage ashrama and has no place for the vanaprastha and the sannyasi.

If we would find the path of return we must be willing to learn from every ancient tradition, from African and Asian tribal religion, from that of the Australian Aborigines and the American Indian. All these people who have been suppressed and almost eliminated by the white races bear within themselves the treasures of the ancient wisdom. By

---

Whatever we do affects everything in the universe.
Lakota wisdom

returning to them we are returning to our own past, to the wisdom of the unconscious which has been suppressed in us, to the heart of the child which is hidden in every man. Our civilisation will remain for ever psychologically unbalanced until it has done justice to these people. The Negro will remain a perpetual challenge to white civilisation until the wisdom which he possesses, the intuitive wisdom of primeval man, has been recognized.
Bede Griffiths[13]

Kenneth Kaunda expresses revulsion at the notion of the Western 'Old People's Home', as a phenomenon unthinkable in traditional African society.

Take, for instance, the traditional African attitude to old people. I remember being horrified on the first occasion I made the acquaintance of that Western phenomenon, the Old People's Home. The idea that the state, or some voluntary agency, should care for the aged was anathema to me, for it almost seems to imply that old people are a nuisance who must be kept out of the way, so that children can live their lives unhampered by their presence. In traditional societies old people are venerated and it is regarded as a privilege to look after them. Their counsel is sought on many matters and, however infirm they might be, they have a valued and constructive role to play in teaching and instructing their grandchildren. Indeed, to deny a grandparent the joy of the company of his grandchildren is a heinous sin. The fact that

---

Understand creation if you would understand the Creator.
St Columbanus

old people can no longer work, or are not alert as they used to
be, or even have developed the handicap of senility in no way
affects our regard for them. We cannot do enough to repay
them for all they have done for us. They are embodied
wisdom, living symbols of our continuity with the past.
Kenneth Kaunda[14]

When I reflect on the stages of life through which we pass,
I sometimes wonder which of those stages is the most critical
in terms of the gathering and sharing of life wisdom. There is
the first quarter of life, when we are young, and live much
more fully in the present moment than we will do as we
grow older. We 'contribute' nothing to the global economy,
and yet we experience life with an immediacy that will soon
fade in the light of common day. Then come the second and
third quarters. We are adults, at the peak of our strength. We
are occupied with the mammoth task of keeping the world
going, maintaining the economy, building our houses, forging
our careers, raising our families. And then comes the final
quarter. We return to a state of dependence. We go back to
living in the 'Now'. There is time to reflect, and to share our
reflections with those who have ears to hear.

In our Western society we shine the spotlight of
significance very heavily on the middle two quarters of life –
the 'achieving years', the 'doing time'. Childhood and old
age are marginalized, as something we will 'grow out of', or
'put up with' respectively. Other societies, and especially
traditional societies, see the balance very differently. The

To turn a battle site into a place of prayer was typical of the
Celtic desire to heal the land, turning darkness to light.
Michael Mitton

precious times, the seasons to cherish and protect, are the first and the last quarters, when wisdom is being seeded and harvested respectively. The middle years serve only to maintain the world so that these crucial processes can be sustained. And so the very young and the very old are regarded as the cradle and the culmination of wisdom, and are given the reverence their role invites.

Just as the elders are the fount of wisdom, so too it is a prime responsibility to pass on this wisdom to those who follow after, and to leave them the legacy of an earth that has been enriched, and not impoverished, by our own lives. This latter duty is vividly expressed in the sacred law of the 'Seventh Generation':

> *In our way of life… with every decision we make, we always keep in mind the Seventh Generation of children to come… When we walk upon Mother Earth, we always plant our feet carefully, because we know that the faces of future generations are looking up at us from beneath the ground. We never forget them.*
> **Oren Lyons**[15]

Only now is the so-called 'first world' beginning to wake up to the dire consequences that we face for having disregarded this wisdom of the 'seventh generation'. In recent centuries white Western culture has spread throughout the world, pushing everything before it like a tidal wave, carried high on the hubris of a belief that our

---

If we would find the path of return we must be willing to learn from every ancient tradition.
Bede Griffiths

way must always be the best way, and must therefore be imposed upon all the earth. Only now do we begin to hear the voices from the 'Third World' (which, of course, is actually the First World, where all humankind has its origins), saying that we may have more to learn from traditional societies than we have to teach them.

It is not by raising Africa to the level of the West that we Africans can answer the world's invitation.

It is not by endowing Africa with every material good that we shall grow.

It is not by integrating Africa into world commerce that we shall hand over to the world what Destiny asks of us.

Certainly Africa must be modernised, and as quickly as possible. Certainly Africa must be enriched. We must work for that with all our strength, not with any ambition to equal or compete with the West, but so that these goods may be a cloak to cover us as we go forward to build up a renewed humanism.

This cloak must cover our own hearts
Our conception of ubuntu (human qualities)
Our love of ubuvyeyi (parental dignity)
Our practice of ubufasoni (nobility of origin)
Our sense of ubutungana (integrity)
The respect for Imana (God) – (our father's legacy to us).
Aylward Shorter[16]

The miracle is not to fly in the air, or to walk on the water, but to walk on the earth.
Chinese proverb

Returning to our roots

In the twentieth century, Western Christianity experienced a time of considerable renewal, in both Protestant and Catholic circles. Invariably, this renewal involved a conscious return to what was recognized as the 'original charism'. Thus, religious orders rediscovered the aspirations and the ideals of their founders, and in doing so rediscovered the source of their own energy and the direction of their particular dream. Many Christians demanded a return to the person of Jesus Christ, whose transforming power can be stifled by the trappings of religion.

The need to 'return to the origin' is always the beginning of growth in our understanding and practice of what it means to be human. Irish priest and prophet Diairmuid Ó'Murchú reminds us that globally too, as a human family, we must rediscover the energy of our origins. I have been present when he has made an impassioned assertion that unless and until the human family re-discovers right relationship with the African continent and peoples, there will be no spiritual progress.

Africa is where we first walked upright; the ancient footsteps are still visible in Tanzania. Africa is where we first used our hands and minds to fashion tools and create ancient art. It is in Africa that we first lifted our hearts and minds to the embracing sense of the divine Spirit. It is in Africa that we discovered fire, speech and spirituality. Africa is a

---

My soul remains quiet; it lives in the other world which no one owns.
Li Po

museum of the human spirit, a treasury of all that is sacred
and dear to the human heart.
Diairmuid Ó'Murchú[17]

What we reap from our collective past, we must also
plant into the future, and the priceless gift of life is nowhere
more tangible than in the newborn child. Traditional
societies celebrate 'rites of passage' in ways that express the
deep awareness of the continuity and sanctity of life, its
dependence upon a sustaining creation. I was fascinated
recently to watch a TV documentary filmed among a
remote hunter-gatherer tribe of people in Tanzania. At the
heart of their village was an ancient baobab tree, completely
hollowed out on the inside by the passage of time. But this
ancient tree witnessed other kinds of 'passage': it was the
birthing tree. The women of the village would go inside it
to give birth, and stay there until the umbilical cord fell
away from the newborn. The documentary showed this vast
tree, with the clouds wheeling above it and the wide African
skies, and superimposed upon this scene were the faces of
some of the community's little ones, who had first seen the
light of day in the depths of this tree.

Thomas Berry describes a birthing ritual of the Omaha
people:

Earlier, Earth was a more intimate reality than it is
at present. Animals and humans were relatives. This
relationship found visible expression in the totemic carvings

---

We live our little story under the great story.
Richard Rohr

discovered throughout the world. The powers of the universe were grandfathers and grandmothers. A pervasive rapport with the spirit powers of the natural world was developed. Ritual enabled humans to enter into the grand liturgy of the universe itself. Seasonal renewal ceremonies brought humans into the rhythms of the solar and lunar cycle. Architectural structures were set on coordinates identified with the position of the heavenly bodies.

We observe this intimate relationship with the universe in the Omaha ceremony carried out at the time of birth. The infant is taken out under the sky and presented to the universe and to the various natural forces with the petition that both the universe and this continent with all their powers, will protect and guide the child toward its proper destiny. In this manner the infant is bonded with the entire natural world as the source, guide, security and fulfilment of life.

Thomas Berry[18]

Esther de Waal, in her exploration of Celtic spirituality and wisdom, describes how a newborn child was greeted in traditional Celtic society, hovering between paganism and Christianity:

When a child was born it was handed to and fro across the fire three times, some words being addressed in an almost inaudible murmur to the fire-god. It was then carried three times sun-wise round the fire, some words being murmured to the sun-god. So at the same time that the child was being

---

**Wisdom, after all, is not a station you arrive at,
but a manner of travelling.**
Sue Monk Kidd

*commended to the Trinity it was also being inserted into
the world of primal elements of fire and water, and its
connectedness to the earth itself was established right away
as it was carried round the hearth in the direction of the
sun's daily movement.*
Esther de Waal[19]

In another book, Esther de Waal notes the close
affinity between Celtic spirituality and traditional African
spirituality, and how both of these approaches to the divine
invited people into an experience of God which was in no
way separated from their experience of everyday living or
any part of their life's journey:

*As I started to read whatever I could about traditional
African spirituality I found extraordinary similarities
[with Celtic spirituality]. For religion both permeated and
informed the whole of life, so that there was no formal
distinction between the sacred and the secular, the
material and the spiritual. In Africa, as in Scotland,
Ireland and Wales centuries ago, religion accompanied
men and women from before birth until after death. It
accompanied them in the house and in the fields. Here
was a religion which did not call men and women out of
their environment, but redeemed them within it.*
Esther de Waal[20]

Among the Aboriginal people of Australia the naming of

**When I return to forever, may the circle be closed
and the spiral broader.**
Marlo Morgan

a person is an ongoing process. A newborn child is named, but only life itself will reveal to the person what form his or her evolving identity will take, and what particular gifts it will embody. A rewarding meditation might be to reflect on what our own name could be: with what special gifts have we been endowed personally, and how have we used them for the good of the wider community; how might that 'name' have changed and evolved through different stages of our lives?

> Each child is named at birth, but it is understood that as a person develops, the birth name will be outgrown, and the individuals will select for themselves a more appropriate greeting. Hopefully, one's name will change several times in a lifetime as wisdom, creativity, and purpose also become more clearly defined with time. Our group contained Story Teller, Tool Maker, Secret Keeper, Sewing Master, and Big Music, among many others.
>
> **Marlo Morgan**[21]

Pain and suffering are vital ingredients in the process of becoming a fully human person. Indigenous peoples have known, and continue to know, more than their fair share of exploitation and abuse. But we don't grow in wisdom simply by experiencing suffering. We grow through what we choose to do with the experience, and how we choose to respond to it. Howard Thurman recognizes that the wisdom of the Negro Spirituals has its roots in harsh experience

---

We are all flowers in the Great Spirit's garden.
Grandfather David Monongye

that has been transformed into a new kind of light:

> Howard Thurman understood the Negro Spirituals as
> connecting creativity and the imago Dei (image of God) in
> humanity. In these songs he saw human creativity and spirit
> at work – a co-working. This is the discovery made by the
> slave that finds its expression in song – a complete and final
> refusal to be stopped. The spirit broods over all the stubborn
> and recalcitrant aspects of experience, until they begin
> slowly but inevitably to take the shape of one's deep
> desiring. There is a bottomless resourcefulness in man that
> ultimately enables him to transform 'the spear of frustration
> into a shaft of light'. Under such a circumstance even one's
> deepest distress becomes so sanctified that a vast
> illumination points the way to the land one seeks.
> **Matthew Fox[22]**

Turning poison into medicine is a process that lies at the
heart of indigenous wisdom, and, indeed, at the heart of
Christian spirituality, in the journey from cruel death to
transcendent life. A friend who is a paramedic, and
encounters life's most desperate and fear-filled situations on
a daily basis once shared with me how he tries, on every
call, to bring a positive attitude into the sickroom, and how
this visibly affects the patient's own feelings and reactions,
often calming the fear and turning desperation into hope.
An American Indian bereavement ritual captures this
possibility.

What makes up a cloud is also what makes up you.
Marlo Morgan

Amerindian man, when he is bereaved, will go into the forest and choose a tree; he will then hit the tree several times with an axe, making a deep wound in the tree. This tree then becomes the man's special place. He identifies the wound in the tree with his own grief. The tree becomes a focus for his grief and whenever he feels the need he will return to the tree simply to be quiet, or to weep, or to remember his loved one who has died. Each time he visits he is confronted by the wound in himself. As time goes by he sees the wound in the tree begin to heal, the sap dries up, and the tree continues to grow, its leaves bud in the spring and die off in the autumn. Despite the wound which has marked the tree for ever, it continues to grow, life goes on. Slowly the Indian begins to heal, certainly the mark remains and he will never be the same again, but his life goes on, the seasons come and go and he continues to grow.
Michael Smith[23]

All of these rites of passage can be understood as expressions of the insight that the human heart is created to be in right relation with all creation, and to hold infinity within itself. This great heart-capacity is a gift that grows by being used. It expands beneath the stars, around the campfire as we share our stories, and on the sacred boundaries between life and death, seed-time and harvest, humankind and God. Conversely, it shrinks if we confine it to the trivia of the shopping malls and the gossip columns. If we would grow in wisdom ourselves, we would do well to tune our

---

To become human one must make room in oneself for the immensities of the universe.
Brian Swimme

inner ear to the voices of our forebears and elders in the human story:

> *The Indians of South America teach that to become human 'one must make room in oneself for the immensities of the universe'. Unless we do so, we cannot find our true nature. We will wander in pain and loneliness. Caught in fragments of our nature, we will attach ourselves to one fragment after another, each taking us further away from our centre.*
> **Brian Swimme**[24]

Perhaps we might give the last word in this section to a Word – the incarnate Word of God, who, in the words of a Jesuit priest working in South Africa, the 'rainbow nation', resonates for him in 'eleven forms of life':

> *IsiZulu, IsiXhosa,*
> *TshiVenda, SeTswana,*
> *XiTsonga, SiSwati,*
> *SePedi, SeSotho,*
> *IsiNdebele, English,*
> *And also Afrikaans – Eleven forms of life*
> *Where words are born*
> *And the Word, who*
> *Slid the rainbow into*
> *Place, comes to welcome*
> *And enlarge the*
> *Question with his answer.*

The soul would have no rainbow if the eyes had no tears.
Native American saying

There is a space where
Language finds a parable –
The Word, who smiles
Now and cries in
Eleven forms of life.
Brian McClorry SJ[25]

Peace is every step.
Native American saying

Desert Wisdom

Very few people who are conscious of their lives as a spiritual as well as a physical journey can say at the end of that journey that the way has not led them through desert terrain at some time. Indeed, in the fourth century AD, the Egyptian deserts became the host to early Christian hermits who chose the path of solitude and extreme privation as a way to approach God more closely. By this time Christianity had become 'official', with the conversion of the Emperor Constantine, and the long process of institutionalization had begun. The flight to the desert was an expression of the desire to dig deeper into the wells of experience and a refusal to remain within the 'comfort zone' of a faith that could easily be deadened by routine.

Desert facts, desert faith, desert feelings

Not all our desert experience is chosen. In fact most of it is something we would do a great deal to avoid if we could see it coming. Even as I write, and you read, these words,

---

**You said live out loud, and die you said lightly,
and over and over again you said be.**
Rainer Maria Rilke

thousands of our fellow human beings, who woke up this morning with bright hopes and a sure agenda, are sitting on the benches of a hospital emergency department, or responding to a knock on the door from the police, to report a sudden death, or to carry out an arrest, or are reeling under the shattering news of a lost job or a broken relationship. The desert can rise up in the midst of a spring morning, to kill our joy and steal our hope. Or it can creep up on us like a deadly fog, day after painful day, until we feel it will suffocate the life out of us.

Can there be any good in such a place from which our hearts instinctively recoil?

On our planet of extremes, perhaps the most frightening and fascinating places are deserts. Covering one-fifth of the earth's land surface, they form the harshest and most barren of environments... Rainfall in most parts of the Sahara is scant and erratic, some areas enduring several years without even a hint of a shower. In common with other desert regions, strong unpredictable winds form typical weather patterns. These winds can blow for days on end, bringing with them vast amounts of dust and sand, which cover everything in their path and reduce visibility down to almost zero. Yet, surprisingly, the Sahara has 1,200 varieties of plants, many only found in the desert.

While physical deserts make up a large part of our physical world, their spiritual equivalents, which we might

When life confronts us with our limits, those who have lived with limits all their lives instruct us most profoundly.
Belden Lane

*call 'spiritual deserts', often make up a large part of many
people's Christian journey... This can often be a long
journey in a wasteland. Yet it can also be a journey of
tremendous value, personal growth, spiritual depth and
encounter with God. For as the physical deserts which
appear so bleak and void contain such a richness of life and
such vastly different species of plant and wildlife, so too the
spiritual deserts contain hidden and often wonderful secrets.*
Alan Jamieson[1]

'Surprisingly,' Jamieson tells us, 'the Sahara has 1,200
varieties of plants.' This fact certainly did surprise me, but
when I went on to read his assurance that the spiritual desert
can likewise be fruitful in ways we could never have predicted,
I knew the truth of his insight. Though usually we need the
benefit of hindsight to see what good things have grown in
our life's deserts, the fact of such growth is undeniable.
Was it this deep knowledge of the spiritual power of the
desert that led Jesus into the desolation of the mountains,
where he faced his own worst fears and temptations?

*And at once the Spirit drove him into the desert and he
remained there for forty days, and was put to the test
by Satan. He was with the wild animals, and the angels
looked after him.*
Mark 1:12–13

Was it for this reason that the people of Israel were led,

That which does not destroy me makes me stronger.
Viktor Frankl

by Moses and by God, into the desert in their flight from
Egyptian oppression?

> *When Pharaoh had let the people go, God did not let them
> take the road to the Philistines' territory, although that was
> the shortest, 'in case', God thought, 'the prospect of fighting
> makes the people change their minds and turn back to
> Egypt.' Instead God led the people a roundabout way
> through the desert of the Sea of Reeds.*
> **Exodus 13:17–18**

It may seem a capricious kind of god who deliberately
leads his beloved people into such a place of hardship,
where they must fight with their own demons and struggle
to survive. Yet this is no capricious god, but the God who
knows that the path to true freedom leads through the
desert of struggle and loss. In the desert times we learn
to observe ourselves and discover who we are, and we
gradually develop the strength to live true to what we
discover. The wisdom of Alcoholics Anonymous reminds
us that:

> *The price of freedom is eternal vigilance.*

We are taught this kind of vigilance, along with many
other things, in our desert times.

The experience always comes as a shock to our
certainties, our expectations and our securities.

**To become a great, cracked, wide-open door
into nowhere is Wisdom.**
May Sarton

Ralph Wright describes it vividly in his poem 'Warshock':

Warshock
on looking at a picture in the Pentagon

wide eyes
stare
out of nobody
into nothing

shell burst
mind burst
blind

like surf
men break
endlessly
on this beach

rippling the sand.
Ralph Wright[2]

When we face our deserts, we too will stare wide-eyed 'out of nobody into nothing'. Any doctor, nurse, or hospital or prison chaplain will know this reaction all too well, as they sit with those who are living through their own personal 'warshock'.

The psalmist knew this desert experience intimately.

**Fierce landscapes remind us that what we long for and
what we fear most are both already within us.**
Belden Lane

Out of the depths I cry to you, O Lord.
Lord, hear my voice!
Psalm 130:1–2

I well remember voicing my own cry for help in these words, during a difficult time, using the words of the Taizé chant, over and over:

> *O Lord, hear my prayer,*
> *O Lord hear my prayer,*
> *Come and listen to me...*

The question comes back to haunt us: can such experience ever be life-giving?

A place of self-discovery

We often hear it said that when disaster strikes you find out who your real friends are. The 'fair-weather friends' mysteriously dissolve into history. We discover who our true companions really are. Even more importantly, we discover who we ourselves really are. When the masks and defences are stripped away, what is underneath them? What does the core of our being look like when its wrappings are removed? For most of us, the desert times are the only way to find out.

Give me a candle of the Spirit, O God, as I go down into the

The soul grows by subtraction, not by addition.
Meister Eckhart

deeps of my being. Show me the hidden things, the creatures of my dreams, the storehouse of forgotten memories and hurts. Take me down to the spring of my life, and tell me my nature and my name. Give me freedom to grow, so that I may become that self, the seed of which you planted in me at my making. Out of the deep I cry to you, O God.
Jim Cotter[3]

This is a dangerous and courageous prayer. It is an expression of willingness to surrender to the power of the desert, to plunge to the depths of the well, not knowing what may await us there. Above all it is an expression of trust, that life will ultimately hold sway over death, and light will prevail over darkness. The desert turns this kind of believing into bedrock faith. It can turn the stones of routine credal believing into living bread to sustain us in the long journey of becoming the people God is dreaming us to be.

In the extreme darkness, we discover what matters to us, what the true essence of our being is really about. The more terrible the darkness, the more sharply focused our self-discovery becomes.

There were grace notes in the unspeakably evil acts of September 11, 2001. No one phoned out of those buildings in hatred or revenge. Instead, the calls and e-mails were an affirmation of life and love: 'I love you; take care of yourself,' 'I love you and the kids. God bless you and good-bye,' or simply, 'You've been a good friend.'

The epiphany on the mountain's height is inseparable from struggle and temptation on the desert floor.
Belden Lane

... if the terrorists' intent was to destroy us, they failed miserably. And we succeeded in finding a measure of grace. A more unified country, at least for a time. No riots, no panicked runs on banks. We were a more thoughtful people, if only briefly. We enjoyed the grace of a week without the usual bombardment of advertisements, a week without celebrity trivia. Now that we've gone back to worrying about what Ben Affleck eats for breakfast and what Jennifer Lopez is wearing, or not wearing, we might recall the seriousness to which we were called on September 11 and find something meaningful there.

Kathleen Norris[4]

And we can see what Kathleen Norris calls 'the aridity of grace' in the worldwide reaction to the disaster of the Asian tsunami in 2004, when a huge outpouring of human compassion became an overwhelming response of financial and practical aid, in which the unconditional generosity of ordinary individuals across the nations far outstripped the measured aid efforts of their governments.

The final messages of the hijack victims of 11 September are an expression of the human capacity to sing in the face of death. This is no easy song. It is the music of a broken heart, but it has the power to resonate with the heart of God and become something eternal. There is a story of a young girl who had a good singing voice. Her parents were uncertain as to whether they should send her for professional training, and so, when she was twelve, they

---

The growth of the spirit is perhaps the most beautiful revelation of God's love that we are privileged to see,

asked a musician friend to assess her gift. He came to audition her, and when she had finished singing, he gave his verdict: 'She sings beautifully,' he said. 'When her heart has been broken she will sing sublimely!' The song that is sung in the face of death is an expression of that sublimity. It is a song of God – the God who is with God's people wherever they are and whatever they experience, constantly transforming the desert into a place of fulfilment:

Recently, many Native Americans have examined the Boarding/Mission School Era of our history in the United States. One of the most striking stories about this period tells of Indian children of the late nineteenth century who were forcibly taken from family and home and sent by train to distant boarding schools. As they were taken away, many of them sang their death songs. Unfortunately, this was no mere exaggeration of childhood fear: some of those children never returned.

In Black Elk's teaching, singing one's own song in the face of death demonstrates the power of the Spirit world… There are stories about Indian warriors from the Plains tribes who would sing their death songs before going into battle. It was seen as the ultimate courage for a human being to sing at that moment.
Marie Therese Archambault[5]

I am told, by those who were present, that there was a dramatic, though silent, outpouring of protest one night

---

and like all beginnings of life, it is about the secret emergence of something new and vulnerable in the darkness.
Sheila Cassidy

during the time of the Communist regime in the former
East Germany. It happened at the opera house, where
Verdi's *Nabucco* was being performed. When the 'Chorus of
the Hebrew Slaves' was sung, everyone in the auditorium
rose to their feet in silent protest – a silence which stated,
more eloquently than words: 'We are captives too, and our
song of freedom shall not be silenced for ever.'

From her experience as a political prisoner in Chile,
Sheila Cassidy describes the most poignant of songs from
the depths of the darkness:

*At about twelve [on Christmas Eve] the priest came and we sat
on benches and on the ground in what shade we could find, for
the sun was very hot, and joined with the priest in the prayers
of the mass. Seldom have I participated in a more moving act
of worship, for we were joined, Christians and Marxists,
believers and atheists, in praise and thanksgiving and desperate
asking to our God or whatever force drives the universe. There
were many tears as we sang familiar hymns and especially the
'Song of Joy' which has become like a protest song in Chile, for
it speaks of the day when all men will again be brothers. At the
communion Georgina carried her baby to the altar with her
and I think there was no one who did not see in Javiera the
defenceless babe of Bethlehem...*

*Then at exactly ten o'clock came the most moving ceremony
I have ever witnessed, for it was the hour which had been set to
sing for the benefit of the men, so near and yet so far, in their
compound a hundred yards away. Standing on tables and benches*

Tell the story, but don't cage the dragon
and charge admission.
Belden Lane

so that their voices would carry further the girls sang as if their lungs would burst and their hearts would break. Their song filled the night air and rose towards the star-filled sky as they sent their Christmas message of love and hope to their menfolk and to those who had no one to love them behind the high concrete wall. On and on they sang, finishing with the mighty chorus of the song written in prison: 'Animo, Negro José'. Take heart, Joe my love.
  Sheila Cassidy[6]

Her experience echoes another 'song in the darkness', from 1914. A true story, which has become a European legend, relates how, on Christmas Eve the opposing German and British forces, lined up against each other in the trenches of northern France, defied the orders of war and celebrated the possibility of peace.

We shook hands, wished each other a Merry Christmas and were soon conversing as if we had known each other for years. We were in front of their wire entanglements and surrounded by Germans... little groups of Germans and British extending almost the length of our front! Out of the darkness we could hear laughter and see lighted matches, a German lighting a Scotsman's cigarette and vice versa, exchanging cigarettes and souvenirs... Here we were laughing and chatting to men whom only a few hours before we were trying to kill... This experience has been the most practical demonstration I have seen of 'Peace on earth towards men'.
  Oswald Tilley[7]

We can make the sorrow and suffering into a compost out of which the roses of joy can grow.
Satish Kumar

This fraternization culminated in the shared singing of the carol '*Stille Nacht*', 'Silent Night', and a celebratory soccer game in No-Man's Land! And it sowed in these men's hearts the question: 'Whose husband, father, brother, son, am I being asked to kill?' When such questions begin to be asked, dawn is breaking in the heart of humanity. What is asked of us is that we stand still in the midst of the pain, and allow the song to transform both the desert, and ourselves.

Stand still in the pain,
Rooted in that in you which is light.
Let the sword go through you.
Maybe it is not
A sword at all.
Maybe it is a tuning fork.
You become a note.
You become the music
You always longed
To hear. You didn't know you were
A song.
Ylva Eggehorn[8]

Refiner's fire

The power of fire to reduce us to our naked core is a much-used metaphor, but also a physical fact. In the bush fires of Australia, for example, only the extreme heat of the

---

Once we ourselves have suffered,
the suffering of others falls upon our softened hearts

flames is able to burst open the seeds of the eucalyptus trees. The conflagration becomes the cradle of new life.

In the life of Oskar Schindler, the 'righteous gentile' whose commitment and courage saved the lives of thousands of Jews who would otherwise have become victims of the Holocaust, we find a story of how the base metal of man's inhumanity to man is refined to gold through the grace of courage, compassion and gratitude. When the nightmare had finally ended, some of the men who owed their lives to Schindler's courageous intervention wanted to make him a gift to express their gratitude:

> All that was readily to hand to make a gift, however, was base metal. It was Mr Jereth who had suggested a source of something better. He opened his mouth to show his gold bridgework. Without Oskar, he said, the SS would have the damned stuff anyway. My teeth would be in a heap in some SS warehouse, along with the golden fangs of strangers from Lublin, Lódz and Lwów.
>
> It was, of course, an appropriate offering and Jereth was insistent. He had the bridgework dragged out by a prisoner who had once had a dental practice in Cracow. Licht the jeweller melted the gold down and by noon on May 8th was engraving a Hebrew inscription on the inner circle of a ring. It was a Talmudic verse which Stern had quoted to Oskar in the front office of Buchheister's in October, 1939. 'He who saves a single life, saves the world entire.'
> **Thomas Keneally**[9]

---

and we become more human members of the human race.
Henri Nouwen

The inscription is from an ancient Jewish text:

*Humankind was originally created as a single individual
[i.e. Adam], to teach that whoever destroys a single human
life, Scripture accounts it to him as if he had destroyed an
entire world, and whoever saves a single human life,
Scripture accounts it to him as if he had saved an entire
world.*
Mishnah Sanhedrin 4:5

Another Holocaust victim, Viktor Frankl, recalls how
the experience of the camps had the capacity to draw out
the very best from those who suffered, to the extent to
which they were willing to choose the path of life rather
than death, of remaining human rather than sinking into
despair. Inspired by the words of Nietzsche, Frankl
asserts:

*Was mich nicht umbringt, macht mich stärker.
(That which does not destroy me makes me stronger.)*

And he describes how this philosophy becomes incarnate
in the facts of concentration camp life:

*We who lived in concentration camps can remember the
men who walked through the huts comforting others, giving
away their last piece of bread. They may have been few in
number, but they offer sufficient proof that everything can*

A crisis is a holy summons to cross a threshold.
Sue Monk Kidd

be taken from a man but one thing: the last of the human freedoms – to choose one's attitude in any given set of circumstances, to choose one's own way.

And there are always choices to make. Every day, every hour, offered the opportunity to make a decision, a decision which determined whether you would or would not submit to those powers which threatened to rob you of your very self, your inner freedom; which determined whether or not you would become the plaything of circumstance, renouncing freedom and dignity to become moulded into the form of the typical inmate.

What was really needed was a fundamental change in our attitude toward life. We had to learn ourselves and, furthermore, we had to teach the despairing men, that it did not matter what we expected from life, but rather what life expected from us.

From all this we may learn that there are two races of men in this world, but only these two – the 'race' of the decent man and the 'race' of the indecent man. Both are found everywhere; they penetrate into all groups of society. No group consists entirely of decent or indecent people. In this sense, no group is of 'pure race' – and therefore one occasionally found a decent fellow among the camp guards. Life in the concentration camp tore open the human soul and exposed its depths. Is it surprising that in those depths we again found only human qualities which in their very nature were a mixture of good and evil? The rift dividing good from evil, which goes through all human beings,

---

**In the final loss of everything that once was sure,
there is also the birth of something new.**
Belden Lane

reaches into the lowest depths and becomes apparent even
on the bottom of the abyss which is laid open by the
concentration camps.
Viktor E. Frankl[10]

The refiner's fire also acts as a powerful focusing light. When we are stripped of everything we thought was so essential to our existence, we discover the nugget of gold that is existence itself. In a contemporary novel, *Life of Pi*, the young boy Pi is trying to survive on a small boat adrift at sea, with a wild tiger on board, whom he names Richard Parker. He describes his attempts to survive emotionally and spiritually in this impossible situation, as he first tries to fight off the desolation with religious ritual, and then seeks to discover the good in the situation, and only when all this fails, does he reach a point of seeing what he calls a single 'shining point of light in my heart'.

I practised religious rituals that I adapted to the circumstances
– solitary Masses without priests or consecrated Communion
hosts, darshans without murtis, and pujas with turtle meat for
Prasad, acts of devotion to Allah not knowing where Mecca
was and getting my Arabic wrong. They brought me comfort,
that is certain. But it was hard, oh, it was hard. Faith in God
is an opening up, a letting go, a deep trust, a free act of love –
but sometimes it was so hard to love. Sometimes my heart
was sinking so fast with anger, desolation and weariness,
I was afraid it would sink to the very bottom of the Pacific

I wonder now if my deep sense of homelessness does not bring
me closer to you than my occasional feelings of belonging.
Henri Nouwen

and I would not be able to lift it back up.

At such moments I tried to elevate myself. I would touch the turban I had made with the remnants of my shirt and I would say aloud, 'THIS IS GOD'S HAT!'

I would pat my pants and say aloud, 'THIS IS GOD'S ATTIRE!'

I would point to Richard Parker and say aloud, 'THIS IS GOD'S CAT!'

I would point to the lifeboat and say aloud, 'THIS IS GOD'S ARK!'

I would spread my hands wide and say aloud, 'THESE ARE GOD'S WIDE ACRES!'

I would point at the sky and say aloud, 'THIS IS GOD'S EAR!'

And in this way I would remind myself of creation and of my place in it.

But God's hat was always unravelling. God's pants were falling apart. God's cat was a constant danger. God's ark was a jail. God's wide acres were slowly killing me. God's ear didn't seem to be listening.

Despair was a heavy blackness that let no light in or out. It was a hell beyond expression. I thank God it always passed. A school of fish appeared around the net or a knot cried out to be reknotted. Or I thought of my family, of how they were spared this terrible agony. The blackness would stir and eventually go away, and God would remain, a shining point of light in my heart. I would go on loving!
Yann Martell[11]

**When you don't transform your pain
you will always transmit it.**
Richard Rohr

Perhaps the beleaguered 'Pi' puts his finger on the heart of the matter. The secret of desert transformation is 'to go on loving'.

This ability to go on loving when the world and its people appear so deeply unloveable is expressed in this final prayer by an unknown victim in Ravensbrück concentration camp:

> O Lord, remember not only the men and women of good will, but also those of ill will. But do not remember all the suffering they have inflicted on us – remember instead the fruits we have bought, thanks to this suffering: our comradeship, our loyalty, our humility, our courage, our generosity, the greatness of heart which has grown out of all this. And when those who have inflicted suffering on us come to judgement, let all the fruits which we have borne be their forgiveness.
>
> **Found on a piece of paper, placed with the body of a dead child in Ravensbrück.**

And so a human heart, speaking for, and from, the extremity of all human experience, re-echoes the words of Jesus from the cross:

> Father, forgive them, for they know not what they do.
> **Luke 23:34**

In Coventry, in the ruins that remained after the destruction of the cathedral and most of the city by enemy

---

Emptiness requires a willingness not to be in control, a willingness to let something new and unexpected happen.

bombers during the Second World War, the inscription
'Father Forgive' is engraved on a cross made of two charred
beams salvaged from the wreckage. I have sometimes stood
and gazed at this inscription, but its full impact only came
home to me when I stood in front of the ruins of Coventry
Cathedral's 'twin', the Frauenkirche in Dresden. For many
years this beautiful church was just a pile of rubble,
destroyed along with almost the whole city of Dresden and
thousands of its people, many of whom were desperate
refugees fleeing from the terror in the East. On 12 February
1945 Dresden was ablaze with firebombs. Its people leapt
into the River Elbe in their attempt to quench the phosphor
flames that engulfed their bodies, but the water only
aggravated their torment. Now the Frauenkirche is restored
– an act of international peace and reconciliation. To be
present there is to hear those words from Coventry re-
echoed: 'Father Forgive', and to feel the pain and the shame
of it in one's own heart.

May Sarton describes these depths of human experience
as a gateway to wisdom:

> *Today, I have learned*
> *That to become*
> *A great, cracked,*
> *Wide-open door*
> *Into nowhere*
> *Is Wisdom.*
> **May Sarton**[12]

It requires trust, surrender and openness to guidance.
God wants to dwell in our emptiness.
Jean Vanier

But there is always a choice about whether or not we are willing to surrender to the process into which the desert times of our living invite us. Moreover, in the desert we are alone with ourselves. There is no one else on whom to project any aspects of ourselves that we would rather not face. In such nakedness, authentic redemption and growth can begin.

The wisdom of the sands is about letting God inform our choices so that we live our lives in harmony with God's will. The secrets of the sands are about containing our projections, and learning the place of strength and the place of weakness, of good and of evil. The desert is both a place and an attitude, but above all it is a task.
Lavinia Byrne[13]

Henri Nouwen summarizes this great human task as a willingness to allow our woundedness to become a source of healing and freedom for others. I had the privilege once of visiting L'Arche Daybreak in Toronto, the community where Nouwen once lived. There the 'broken' and the 'whole' live side by side. I remember especially Maria, a young woman with multiple learning difficulties, who was making a lovely mosaic picture in the workshop there. She was carefully and lovingly piecing it together using broken bits of pottery, and as she worked, she was inwardly re-making, and 're-membering' – putting together again – her own experience of brokenness into a new picture that was

---

Our task is not to shape reality, but to accept and discover within it a light, a new love, a presence.
Desmond Tutu

full of meaning and of hope, not just for herself, but for all who would see it. I watched her with tears in my eyes.

Making one's own wounds a source of healing does not call for a sharing of superficial personal pains but for a constant willingness to see one's own pain and suffering as rising from the depth of the human condition which all men share...
Henri Nouwen[14]

The desert blooms
When the regime of apartheid finally ended in South Africa, and the first democratic elections were held, Desmond Tutu observed the effects at the voting booths, and witnessed a miraculous transformation.

The people had come out in droves and they looked so utterly vulnerable. It would have taken just two or three people with AK-47s to sow the most awful mayhem. It did not happen. What took place can only be described as a miracle. People stood in those long lines, people of all races in South Africa that had known separation and apartheid for so long – black and white, coloured and Indian, farmer, labourer, educated, unschooled, poor, rich – they stood in those lines and the scales fell from their eyes. South Africans made an earth-shattering discovery – hey, we are all fellow South Africans...

Behind every Gandhi, every Mother Teresa, every Romero, every Mandela, there are millions of people who are living lives of love and heroism.
Desmond Tutu

People entered the booth one person and emerged on the other side a totally different person. The black person went in burdened with all the anguish of having had his or her dignity trampled underfoot and being treated as a non-person – and then voted. And said, 'Hey, I'm free – my dignity has been restored, my humanity has been acknowledged. I'm free!' She emerged a changed person, a transformed, a transfigured person.

The white person entered the booth one person, burdened by the weight of guilt for having enjoyed many privileges unjustly, voted, and emerged on the other side a new person. 'Hey, I'm free. The burden has been lifted. I'm free!' She emerged a new, a different, a transformed, a transfigured person. Many white people confessed that they too were voting for the first time – for the first time as really free people. Now they realized what we had been trying to tell them for so long, that freedom was indivisible, that they would never be free until we were free.

Desmond Tutu[15]

The terrible irony is that it is often the desert experience that prepares our hearts for this kind of transformation. It's as though the cutting edge of experience needs to plough up the heart's soil, before the seeding of new growth can begin, and this ploughing is sometimes accompanied by extreme pain. Yet, the new growth does happen, and in the fullness of time, the desert can bloom.

Once, on a journey in the desert, I was amazed when a

Failure was the most valuable truth the desert monastery had to teach me. Disillusionment marks every new beginning in the spiritual life.
Belden Lane

Bedouin guide showed us a tiny, dried-up seed that he picked up from the arid desert sand. He spat on the little seed, and then the miracle happened. Before our eyes, the seed began to sprout! The incident gave me real hope that the dried up seeds inside us can also sprout into new life, but this often happens when we are, so to speak, spat upon by our circumstances. The seed sprang to life in minutes. Our own resurrections can take a lifetime – or longer! The timescale is not ours to fathom. Yet the pattern is as true for us as for that little seed.

Etty Hillesum, a young Jewish girl trying to live her life in Holland as the shadow of the Holocaust deepened and darkened around her, describes her own awareness of life growing in the dark shadow of death:

Yes, the trees, sometimes at night their branches would bow down under the weight of the fruit of the stars, and now they are menacing daggers piercing the bright spring air. Yet even in their new shape and setting they are unspeakably beautiful. I remember a walk along an Amsterdam canal, one dreamlike summer night, long, long ago. I had visions then of ruined cities. I saw old cities vanish and new cities arise, and I thought to myself, even if the whole of this world is bombed to bits, we shall build a new world, and that one too will pass, and still life will be beautiful, always beautiful.

The jasmine behind my house has been completely ruined by the rains and storms of the last few days; its white blossoms are floating about in muddy black pools on the low

---

We achieve our deepest progress standing still.
Sue Monk Kidd

*garage roof. But somewhere inside me the jasmine continues
to blossom undisturbed, just as profusely and delicately as
ever it did. And it spreads its scent round the House in which
you dwell, O God. You can see, I look after you, I bring you
not only my tears and my forebodings on this stormy, grey
Sunday morning. I even bring you scented jasmine. And I
shall bring you all the flowers I shall meet on my way, and
truly there are many of those. I shall try to make You at home
always. Even if I should be locked up in a narrow cell and a
cloud should drift past my small barred window, then I shall
bring you that cloud, O God, while there is still the strength
in me to do so. I cannot promise You anything for tomorrow,
but my intentions are good, You can see.*

Etty Hillesum[16]

Etty never returned from Auschwitz.

Brian Keenan, on the other hand, did survive his ordeal
as a hostage in the Middle East, to describe the experience
in his book *An Evil Cradling*. For him the desert blooms
momentarily in the transfigured appearance of a single
orange. The moment becomes eternal.

*I look at this food I know to be the same as it has always
been.*

*But wait. My eyes are almost burned by what I see.
There's a bowl in front of me that wasn't there before. A
brown button bowl and in it some apricots, some small
oranges, some nuts, cherries, a banana. The fruits, the*

Only love is big enough to hold all the pain of this world.
Sharon Salzberg

colours, mesmerize me in a quiet rapture that spins through
my head. I am entranced by colour. I lift an orange into the
flat filthy palm of my hand and feel and smell and lick it.
The colour orange, the colour, the colour, my God the colour
orange. Before me is a feast of colour. I feel myself begin to
dance, slowly, I am intoxicated by colour. I feel the colour in
a quiet somnambulant rage. Such wonder, such absolute
wonder in such an insignificant fruit.

I cannot, I will not eat this fruit. I sit in quiet joy, so
complete, beyond the meaning of joy. My soul finds its own
completeness in that bowl of colour. The forms of each fruit.
The shape and curl and bend all so rich, so perfect. I want
to bow before it, loving that blazing, roaring, orange
colour... Everything meeting in a moment of colour and of
form, my rapture no longer an abstract euphoria. It is there
in that tiny bowl, the world recreated in that broken bowl.
I feel the smell of each fruit leaping into me and lifting me
and carrying me away. I am drunk with something that I
understand but cannot explain. I am filled with a sense of
love. I am filled and satiated by it. What I have waited and
longed for has without my knowing come to me, and taken
all of me.

This mystical experience of the orange is far more than a
fleeting moment of heightened awareness. It is a door that
opens into a whole new depth of insight, as he goes on to
reflect.

Dark times are among the best teachers.
Richard Rohr

When fear commands the mind then the heart is imprisoned. In time I came to understand the greater and more profound prison that held our captors. For years we were chained to a wall or radiator, but they were chained to their guns; futile symbols of power, not power itself. This was something these men could never know: real power embraces; it cannot destroy.
Brian Keenan[17]

Perhaps the truth is that it is in the nature of God always and everywhere to be seeking to bring life out of whatever humankind presents. The desert blooms, in God's time, not ours, and its fruitfulness depends on two things: our surrender to the pain of the ploughing, and our willingness to be open to the seeding. When these two things come together, the place of suffering can become a place of creativity and growth…

The urge to create something lovely burned like a fire in all the prisons. Underfed and lonely in the snows of Dawson Island the first political prisoners of the Junta, lawyers, doctors, professors and cabinet ministers produced engraved pendants of a haunting loveliness from the finely polished stones that they picked up from the ground under their feet. Later, the men of Chacabuco, the big concentration camp in the northern desert of Chile, produced copper rings made from the wire that had imprisoned them, and engraved pendants from worthless coins.
Sheila Cassidy[18]

When fear commands the mind then the heart is imprisoned.
Brian Keenan

… poison can be turned into medicine…

*Just as some of the purest and most cleansing substances
come from things that are rotten – wine and alcohol from
fermented fruit, penicillin from mould – and just as the
earth is nourished by animal manure, so our hearts and
inner brokenness are healed through communion with all
that we have rejected and are afraid of: the poor and weak,
enemies and strangers.*
Jean Vanier[19]

… captivity can be transformed into a deeper inner
freedom…

*My containment does not oppress me. I sit and look at
the walls but now this room seems so expansive, it seems
I can push the walls away from me, I can reach out and
touch them from where I sit and yet they are so far from
me.*
Brian Keenan[20]

… and experience, in the embrace of patience and
reflectiveness, can mature into wisdom…

*Be patient toward all that is unsolved in your heart and try
to love the questions themselves. Do not now seek answers,
which cannot be given you because you would not be able
to live them. And the point is, to live everything, live the*

**We can't be creative if we refuse to be confused.
Great ideas appear in the space of not knowing.**
Margaret Wheatley

questions now. Perhaps you will gradually, without noticing it, live along some distant day into the answer.
Rainer Maria Rilke[21]

In every desert situation there is a potential for growth. Our choices play a part in determining whether that potential is fulfilled, even though we may never see the harvest of the seeds that were sown in our anguish. Nevertheless we can trust the wisdom of an anonymous first-century philosopher:

When I light a candle at midnight, I say to the darkness: I beg to differ.

Be patient toward all that is unsolved in your heart.
Rainer Maria Rilke

Guiding Wisdom

Wherever and however we begin our journey through life, we stand on giants' shoulders. For thousands of years, humankind has been searching and sifting, recollecting, reflecting, and seeking to pass on the distillation of a lifetime's experience to those who follow after. The result is a gold mine of nuggets of wisdom, and each of us could create our own treasury. In this section we will explore just a few of the pearls of wisdom that the giants who have gone ahead of us have left us as a legacy.

But of course, as in any field, not all we discover from the guidance of others is sound or true. Each of us must discern for ourselves what resonates with our heart's experience, what 'rings true'. The kind of guiding wisdom that liberates us will always come 'free' – that is, without any hidden agenda, of making gain from us, or hooking us in to someone else's spiritual path.

There is enough wisdom on the planet to illuminate every aspect of what it means to be human. Here we will be content to reflect on what just a few wise voices have

---

For everything there is a season, for every task someone is given the tools.
Joan Chittister

had to say about God, about the spiritual quest, about love and relationship, work and creativity, justice and vulnerability, and on the art of being open-hearted and the gift of letting go. May this little aperitif encourage you to explore the feast of wisdom hidden in your own life's treasury.

On God

One thing that most people would agree about is that God is always bigger than all our images of God. In fact our images of God can be a major block to our spiritual growth, especially if we get stuck with them and mistake them for the reality. One of my own favourite descriptions of God comes from the Irish poet Patrick Kavanagh:

God is in the bits and pieces of Everyday –
A kiss here and a laugh again, and sometimes tears,
A pearl necklace round the neck of poverty.
Patrick Kavanagh[1]

An 'everyday God', present in all things, and yet a presence that can disturb us and wrench us out of our comfort zones. The Sufi mystic, Hafiz warns us that our human instinct may well be to flee when we sense God's disturbing presence in our lives, even though that disturbance may well prove to be 'a great favour':

You cannot solve problems with the way of thinking
that led to their creation.
Albert Einstein

Love wants to reach out and manhandle us,
Break all our teacup talk of God…
The Beloved sometimes wants
To do us a great favour:
Hold us upside down
And shake all the nonsense out.
But when we hear
He is in such a 'playful drunken mood'
Most everyone I know
Quickly packs their bags and hightails it
Out of town.
Hafiz[2]

In a contemporary novel by Alice Walker, *The Color Purple*, Shug, a black slave descendant in the American South, speaks of her sense of God, and how she needed to rid herself of the inherited image of the 'old man with a white beard':

She say, Celie, tell the truth, have you ever found God in church? I never did. I just found a bunch of folks hoping for him to show. Any God I ever felt in church I brought in with me. And I think all the other folks did too. They come to church to share God, not find God…

She say, My first step from the old white man was trees. Then air. Then birds. Then other people. But one day when I was sitting quiet and feeling like a motherless child, which I was, it come to me: that feeling of being part of everything,

---

Beyond the boundaries that appear to divide us
is a divine gravity that holds us fast.
Robert Kirschner

not separate at all. I knew that if I cut a tree, my arm would
bleed. And I laughed and I cried and I run all round the
house.
Alice Walker[3]

During a visit to the west of Canada I once bought a little
box of rock fragments purporting to be 'The Canadian
Rockies'. The contents of this little plastic box are beautiful
in themselves – pebbles of many different types, colours
and textures of the rocks that make up the Rocky Mountain
range. I'm glad to have them, but I am in no danger of
confusing the contents of one little box of pebbles with the
vast splendour of the Rocky Mountains themselves. Every
time I see my little box, I am reminded of how very little we
can hold in the tiny, finite boxes of our minds of the vast
mystery of life in this universe.

God is more than everything that has been revealed. He is
like a mighty and ever-flowing river, whereas that which has
been revealed is like a pot of water from the river; a pot of
water cut off from the living river is dead – it begins to
stagnate. People who are hungry and thirsty for the living
water have to go to the river to drink each day. No one can
gather enough living water for his or her whole life. God
gives living water only for today.
John Martin Sahajananda[4]

Where is God? Gerard Hughes asks this question in his

Let's be patient and trust that the treasure we look for
is hidden in the ground on which we stand.
Henri Nouwen

book *God, Where are You?* and answers it by reflecting in depth on his own life's journey and all it has revealed. When signing my copy of his book, the author added, under the title on the front page, the words 'Wherever you happen to be'. His answer is the answer that holds true for all of us. God is in the events of our everyday living, always nudging us closer to the best we can be. Gerard Hughes ends this book with a prayer:

> *Now I know that You are always greater than anything I can think or imagine, and for this I am most grateful. I am glad that I cannot locate You, define You, describe You. I used to worry about self-identity, about who I was. Now I am glad not to know, and I can thank You for the Mystery of my being... But what I do know is that You are the God of every situation, God in the darkness drawing us to light, God in our sinfulness offering us healing, God in our self-deception leading us into truth, God who is for us, even when we are against ourselves. So I know that even if I am unwittingly deceiving myself, if I follow what truth there is in me, then You will draw me further into Your truth, and that there is no situation, no state, no place I can reach where You will not still be closer to me than I am to myself.*
> **Gerard Hughes[5]**

And of Jesus of Nazareth, the purest image of the living God, Kahlil Gibran has this to say.

Don't let the past dictate who you are, but let it become part of who you will become.
From the script of My Big Fat Greek Wedding

*He knew the source of our older self, and the persistent
thread of which we are woven.*

*The Greek and Roman orators spoke to their listeners
of life as it seemed to the mind. The Nazarene spoke of
a longing that lodged in the heart.*

*They saw life with eyes only a little clearer than yours
and mine. He saw life in the light of God.*

*I often think that he spoke to the crowd as a mountain
would speak to the plain.*
Kahlil Gibran[6]

Jesus is the one who can take us on the longest journey
– the journey from the head to the heart. He is the one
who sees deep below external appearance, who sees
everyone with God's eyes, and speaks to us all down the
centuries not from 'above', but as a Presence who both
dwarfs us and raises us up to glimpse the fullness of
everything humanity has the potential to become.

Michael Mayne sees Jesus as the one who

*...alone of all our race looked full at the transcendent
mystery and said his name was Father.*
Michael Mayne[7]

And Rainer Maria Rilke captures something of the very
essence of the divine, the presence who is unique for each
of us, and touches the deepest core of our being in ways
that can transform us:

**Peaceful living is about trusting those on whom we depend
and caring for those who depend on us.**
Dalai Lama

You are the deep innerness of all things,
the last word that can never be spoken.
To each of us you reveal yourself differently:
To the ship as coastline, to the shore as a ship.
Rainer Maria Rilke[8]

On the spiritual quest

What does the spiritual quest mean for *you*? Perhaps we
would all have a different response to offer. For some it
would be formalized in a religious tradition, for others it
would run free and unfettered, and there would be all
shades of experience in between. My own spiritual quest
has often seemed like 'trying to take a close-up photo of
the horizon' – frustrating, riveting, challenging, consoling
and forever stretching me 'to more than I can be'. It has
led me, in the words of the psalmist 'beside still waters',
but it has also led me to the edge of the chasm, where I
have discovered for myself, as Indiana Jones once did, that
when you step out into the abyss – and *only* then – the
bridge will appear.

Many contemporary pilgrims would see a distinction
between spirituality and religion. Traditional organized
religious practice seems to be on the wane, at least in
most traditions in the Western world, and yet there is
undoubtedly a marked surge of interest in 'spirituality'.

Being spiritual is not the same as being religious. Religion is

---

We are only truly grateful people when we can say thank you
to all that has brought us to the present moment.
Henri Nouwen

*about what you believe and do. Spirituality is to do with
quality; it is a thing of the heart. Religion draws lines.
Spirituality reads between them. It tends to avoid
definitions, boundaries and battles. It is inclusive and
holistic. It crosses frontiers and makes connections. It is
characterised by sensitivity, gentleness, depth, openness,
flow, feeling, quietness, wonder, paradox, being, waiting,
acceptance, awareness, healing and inner journey.*
Brian Woodcock[9]

Nevertheless, many still search for the mountain-top
experience that will leave them in no doubt about the
existence and power of the divine, while all the while the
clues to the divine presence are more likely to be found
in the small moments of wonder, and the little pointers
towards transcendence that are so easily overlooked because
they are embedded in everyday experience.

*The turning points in life arrive as small signals at first;
these only amplify when you choose to follow them. So
being vigilant about tiny clues is a major part of spiritual
evolution...*

*When you feel you have been touched by grace, that is
your clue that God exists and cares about what happens
to you...*

*Do not think that when you speak of God, you are near
him. Your words have created the gap that you must cross to
get back to him, and you will never cross it with your mind...*

**Wisdom is not having all the right answers,
it is having all the right questions.**
Neale Donald Walsch

A spiritual person is a good listener for silent voices, a sharp observer of invisible objects. These traits are more important than trying to act in a way that God would reward with a gold star.
Deepak Chopra[10]

A paradox of the journey is that it may challenge us to let go of the need for 'answers' and instead to allow God to put our lives constantly in question. While this is a very uncomfortable and challenging place to be, it may well be a place that leads more directly to the simple heart of the matter than any number of doctrines can do. Every new 'answer' expands the question, just as when you are in a mountainous landscape, you can clearly see the mountain from a distance, and wonder at its beauty, but the closer you get to it, the less of it you see, until finally you are on the rock face and you see almost nothing at all.

Religion does not provide answers to life's questions; it puts our lives in question. It places before us possibilities of action in relation to that which is of infinite value. That is why the questioning, the facing up to such questions, is more important than any specific answer we might, probabilistically and speculatively, come up with…
So it might be possible to cultivate a sort of spirituality, a discipline of the mind and heart, without reliance on controversial doctrines and abstract theological problems. And if we do so, we might find, to our surprise, that what

---

I am not called to be successful, I am called to be faithful.
Mother Teresa of Calcutta

we are doing is to penetrate to the heart of prayer, and of
what genuine belief in God really means...

To believe in God is to give yourself to goodness, to
affirm, in a leap of faith, that the claim of goodness is
absolute, and to commit yourself without reserve to the
power of its presence and the possibility of its actualisation
in the world.

Keith Ward[11]

Our spiritual quest has been a characteristic of what it
means to be human since the earliest beginnings of the
human family. Long before organized religion came on the
scene, humankind had been reaching out to connect in
some way to the profound mystery that held, and holds, all
life in being. Our early ancestors watched the stars, noticed
the heavenly movements, and erected burial chambers, like
that at Newgrange in Ireland, and pyramids, as in Egypt,
as a way of trying to reflect on earth something of the
mysteries of the heavens. They sought to express their
response to life in ancient cave paintings, they developed
rituals to honour the great rites of passage in their lives,
and they honoured special sacred places, such as Uluru
in Australia or the stone circles of Celtic Britain and Ireland,
as places of close encounter with the Author of their being.
In many ways they were more deeply connected to God in
their primitive lifestyles than we are today with all our
sophistication.

Prayer is the bridge between our conscious
and unconscious lives.
Henri Nouwen

Spirituality is written into the weaving and unweaving tapestry of evolution and creation. Our prehistoric ancestors behaved spiritually because they remained connected to the cosmic womb of life, which itself is innately spiritual. It is only by reconnecting with that primordial source – as millions are striving to do today (often in confusing and contradictory ways) – that we can hope to regain our spiritual, planetary and cosmic dignity as a human species.
Diairmuid Ó'Murchú[12]

On loving and relating

All spiritual traditions would agree that however we imagine God to be, God would be the source of Love. Christians would say categorically that 'God is Love', and the Taizé chant reminds us that 'where there is love, there is God' (*Ubi caritas, Deus ibi est*).

So our own efforts at being in loving relationship with each other are clearly a vital aspect of the spiritual quest, and there is no shortage of guidance on how human beings should love one another.

Love is revealed in small steps as well as in extravagant gestures, and small steps are within the reach of all of us.

We choose love by taking small steps of love every time there is an opportunity. A smile, a handshake, a word of encouragement, a phone call, a card, an embrace, a kind greeting, a gesture of support, a moment of attention, a

---

Often in the folds of contradiction is a Great Harmony found.
Neale Donald Walsch

helping hand, a present, a financial contribution, a visit –
all these are little steps toward love.

Each step is like a candle burning in the night. It does
not take the darkness away, but it guides us through the
darkness. When we look back after many small steps of
love, we will discover that we have made a long and
beautiful journey.
Henri Nouwen[13]

Love multiplies by division. Like a bright candle flame
from which many other candles can be lit, so love spreads
by being given away. The paradox of love, and of the
journey with God, is that we are only rich in what we give
away. In 1990, just after the so-called 'Velvet Revolution'
had toppled the totalitarian regime in the Czech Republic,
I had the privilege of experiencing the first Easter Vigil freely
permitted in the Jesuit church in Prague. At the beginning
of the service, the church was in total darkness, recalling
the forty years of suppression and oppression from which
the country had so recently been freed. Then hundreds of
people in the pews lit their tapers from the great paschal
candle, and gradually the church became radiant, not just
with candlelight, but with a palpable sense of hope and joy.
The paschal flame was not diminished, but multiplied, by
being divided like this.

The only thing that one has is what one gives away. By
spending oneself, one becomes rich. And once you've thrown

Do not seek to follow in the footsteps of the Masters:
seek what they sought.
Zen saying

overboard everything, there's one thing left: the only thing
left is the love you've given or the love you give. That was
probably the most important lesson in my life.
Isabel Allende[14]

The love revealed in the life and death of Jesus of
Nazareth is precisely this quality of loving, and is
revolutionary beyond description. Perhaps one of the big
mistakes of organized Christianity is that, by and large, it
seems to underestimate the radical nature of Jesus, with
the result that all too often, his earth-upturning story is
packaged in far too small a box, and offered to the faithful,
tamed and domesticated.

When you think about it, what Christ said two thousand
years ago is extraordinarily radical. He came to a warrior
society where might was right. In most parts of the world it
was still an eye for an eye and a tooth for a tooth. And he
said the most extraordinary things. He said, 'Blessed are the
meek.' What was he talking about? 'Blessed are the poor.'
Who does he think he is? 'Turn the other cheek.' At the time
these were absurd ideas, and yet they're about the only ideas
that make sense if a lot of people are going to live together
on an increasingly crowded planet with diminishing
resources. It's a profound sense. It's a newness.
Melvyn Bragg[15]

In the radically new relationship opened up by Jesus

A gentle person knows that true growth
requires nurture not force.
Henri Nouwen

between God and humankind, and among humankind, the ways of violence are simply not feasible. In his death and resurrection, Jesus himself goes through the 'eye of the needle', into what appears to be his own destruction, but comes through that narrow way into a fullness of life that we cannot begin to imagine. Jesus' self-giving is crystallized in the Christian celebration of the Eucharistic meal – a commemoration of the last supper Jesus shared with his friends, and at which he revealed that he was about to give his whole self, his life, his body and his blood, as an invitation to all to enter into a new relationship with the Source of our being, the living God, whom he called 'Abba' (Father, or simply 'Dad').

Eucharist isn't just a ritual that happens on the altar. It happens whenever there is self-giving, for the sake of another.

A beautiful folk story tells of a sunflower who grew alone on a piece of derelict land. One day a sparrow came to her, and told her how beautiful she was. The two became friends, and every morning the sparrow came to talk to the sunflower. Then one morning he was absent. Days passed, and eventually a weak and dying sparrow came to say his last goodbye to his sunflower friend. In her distress, she bent down to him, and dropped a few of her seeds for him, so that he found a new lease of life. Days passed again, and weeks, and one day the sparrow came to his friend, and was distraught to find that she was dying. 'Don't be dismayed,' she reassured him. 'My time is over, but see, I leave you all

---

Discernment is a way of sifting through our desires and passions, so that our lives may be shaped by the best of them.
David Lonsdale

my seeds. Eat your fill, and let them make you strong,
to survive the winter, but leave a few seeds here on this
ground. Then next year, there will be more sunflowers here
in this wasteland, and more sparrows will fly among them,
and all creation will be enriched.'

I have sometimes told this story to elderly people who
often feel they are useless and unvalued. In doing so, my
hope is that they will realize how many seeds their lives
have sown in the world, even though they may never see
the harvest. Often they have given their life energy and their
love for others unstintingly, and in doing so, they too echo
the words of Jesus 'This is my body, given for you.' They
too are Eucharist.

When I think of the Eucharist (which means 'thanksgiving')
I am reminded of a beautiful story related by a friend of mine,
that happened when he was a young boy and had been very
ill, and was now recovering, and walking on the moors with
his father:

*It was a heavenly day, and Dad and I were quick to share
our delight with one another as first one then another
would come upon a further fresh cluster of the bright black
beauties. And I myself was bathed not only in the warmth of
the sun but also in the warmth and tenderness of my father,
whose heart was visibly rejoicing that his son was now
restored to him. All the same, my strength had not yet fully
returned. So by midday it was a tired boy who agreed to his
father's suggestion that we should put down our brimming*

**It's not differences that divide us. It's our
judgments about each other that do.**
Margaret Wheatley

*carrier bags and sit on the railway embankment to eat our
lunch.*

*No sooner were we sitting on the coarse grass than I
took out my apple and with scarcely a pause for breath
proceeded to eat it, every bit of it apart from the pips. All
the while I was doing so my father sat watching me, an
amused smile on his lips, as he unhurriedly polished his
own apple on his shirt.*

*When he saw that I had spat out the last of the pips he
said to me, 'You were right hungry, lad!' 'Yes, I was,' I
heartily agreed. Whereupon my father said, 'Well, would
you like half of my apple as well?' 'No, Dad,' I answered,
almost indignantly, 'You're hungry as well.' My father
looked at me, his fine honest eyes filled with love; and
speaking in a deep, contented voice he assured me, 'No,
I'm not really.'*

*Of course, I knew that he was. But I also sensed that he
had long since mastered his hunger. Strong man that he
was, he then took the apple into his hands, which had
become cut and calloused over the years through his work,
and he very deliberately broke the apple in two. And even
now, before my mind's eye, I can see the shining white flesh
of the halves of that broken apple, each half resting between
the thick muscles of my father's thumb and forefinger. He
placed one half into my hands and we ate in silence. This
time I ate slowly and deliberately. Something had changed
as a result of which the whole world had become a different
place; it could never be the same again.*

God of goodness, give me yourself,
for you are enough for me.
Julian of Norwich

*In those days, only a child of seven, I could clearly not
have ventured any explanation of that sacred action in
which my father had served as the priest. But the course of
life since has made me realise how, on that abandoned-
looking railway embankment, I had been touched at the
centre of my being, in my very substance, at a level far
deeper than the consciousness of a seven-year-old could
fathom. And nothing would be the same again. That is the
effect of communion.*

Donald Nicholl[16]

On doing and being

From an early age our children tend to be plied with the
question 'What are you going to do when you grow up?'
The result is that we grow up valuing ourselves and each
other very much in terms of 'what we do'. Those who feel
they don't 'do' anything, or at least anything that has an
imposing job title, can become dismissive of themselves
and their own gifts and skills. And those who are 'gainfully
employed', but lose this employment or retire from it, often
suffer from a similar sense of uselessness.

The voices of wisdom tell a rather different story. Work
and creativity are valued gifts of humankind, they would
assure us, but they aren't everything. Who we *are* is
ultimately more important and more permanent than what
we *do*. Though, of course, the two facets of our living are
intertwined in a dynamic partnership. Who we are affects

**Those who speak do not know;
those who know do not speak.**
Tao te Ching

what we do, and the essence of our personality is expressed in what we make and how we act. The skills and gifts we have are to be used not just for our own gain or satisfaction, but for the benefit of the whole of humanity.

We have received a treasure house of traditions as a free gift. In return we offer our work, our creativity, our arts and crafts, our agriculture and architecture as gifts to society – to present and future generations. When we are motivated by this spirit then work is not a burden. It is not a duty. It is not a responsibility. We are not even the doers of our work. Work flows through us and not from us. We do not even own our intellect, our creativity, or our skills. We have received them as a gift and grace. We pass them on as a gift and grace; it is like a river which keeps flowing. All the tributaries make the river great. We are the tributaries adding to the great river of time and culture, the river of humanity.
Satish Kumar[17]

When we live true to who we really are, true to the best in us, then what we do will indeed be for the greater good of all creation, but this is a challenge that we face in every choice we make, moment by moment.

I feel that everything I do has an effect on the world, and I feel empowered, and I feel this energy that is not wasted and

---

Many times the Christ has come to the world, and He has walked many lands.

is not passive. And it's not about suffering. It's about doing positive good things – with a tremendous hope that it has an effect.
Isabel Allende[18]

I am convinced that we can choose joy. Every moment we can decide to respond to an event or a person with joy instead of sadness… To choose joy does not mean to choose happy feelings or an artificial atmosphere of hilarity. But it does mean the determination to let whatever takes place bring us one step closer to the God of life.
Henri Nouwen[19]

I know a place where there is a particularly beautiful little pool hidden away in the woods. It catches the light, seemingly in all weathers, and sparkles even when there is little to sparkle about. Throw a pebble into this pool and you will create a living dance – rings of light and life as the water ripples gently to the edges. We can make choices to bring about this effect in everything we do. We can choose to add life to every situation if we enter it with a positive attitude, expecting the best from it. Or we can go about our daily living as if we were at war with life, always expecting the worst outcome and generating destructive energy that will agitate everything and everyone around us.

Our choices make us who we are, and help to shape the world into all it might become, for good or ill.

And always He has been deemed a stranger and a madman.
Kahlil Gibran

Serve Life first, in everything you think and say and do. Ask yourself, 'Is this thought life-enhancing or life-depleting? Is this word life-enriching or life-detracting? Is this action life-supporting or life-damaging?'
Neale Donald Walsch[20]

There is a great sadness in failing to become what we have the potential to be. One interpretation of the word 'sin' is 'unripeness' – a failure to develop and blossom into the person God dreams us to be, or even the person we ourselves dream we could become. All parenting, all education, at its best, has this great goal, to facilitate the coming-to-maturity of an individual life with its unique endowment of gifts.

All too often this coming-to-be is aborted through the acts, or the neglect, of others. One of my most poignant experiences was a visit to a little cemetery in Berlin where Hans, a young boy of fifteen, was buried back in 1945. He had gone out into the streets, armed only with sticks and stones to defend his native town against the incoming Russian armies, and he had been blown to pieces by a Russian tank. His grave was easy to find. It was bare, except for one small item. From the leafing tree just above it, where a bird had built her nest, a solitary egg had fallen, and its shell lay, broken, on Hans' grave. The broken shell of a tiny bird who would never fly – lying on the grave of a young boy who would never know the fullness of his life. I wept.

God is at home; it is we who have gone out for a walk.
Meister Eckhart

Anyone who is the downfall of one of these little ones would be better drowned in the depths of the sea with a great millstone round his neck.
Matthew 18:6

One way of aborting the coming-to-life of the person we are called to be is to spend our lives trying to be someone else! Perhaps we feel that 'who we are' is just not good enough, or fails to meet the expectations we think others are placing upon us.

On his deathbed Rabbi Zuscha was asked what he thought life beyond the grave would be like. The old man thought for a long time; then he replied: 'I don't really know. But one thing I do know: when I get there I am not going to be asked "Why weren't you Moses?" or "Why weren't you David?" I am going to be asked "Why weren't you Zuscha?"'
Francis Dewar[21]

Simply 'to be' requires a great skill, however: it requires us to develop the ability to live in the present moment. We spend most of our youth living in the future, with all the hopes and anxieties that brings, and then we spend our declining years living in the past, with our memories and our regrets. How rarely we truly and fully live in the moment where we are – perhaps only when we are in love, or when we are wholly engrossed in something we love doing, or when we are taken out of ourselves by a moment

---

The problem with the rat race is that even if you win, you're still a rat.
Neale Donald Walsch

of breathtaking beauty. To cultivate the gift of living in the present moment is something that is urged by all spiritual mentors.

Peace is present right here and now, in ourselves and in everything we do and see. The question is whether or not we are in touch with it. We don't have to travel far away to enjoy the blue sky. We don't have to leave our city or even our neighbourhood to enjoy the eyes of a beautiful child. Even the air we breathe can be a source of joy...

Every breath we take, every step we make, can be filled with peace, joy, and serenity. We need only to be awake, alive in the present moment.
Thich Nhat Hanh[22]

If we can only live fully in the moment, then we will be able:

> *To see a world in a grain of sand,*
> *And a heaven in a wild flower,*
> *Hold infinity in the palm of your hand*
> *And eternity in an hour.*
> **William Blake**[23]

The gift of an open heart
The spiritual quest is always going to draw us beyond ourselves. This is the secret of transcendence – to trust that

---

The soul grows by subtraction, not by addition.
Meister Eckhart

God is always greater than we can imagine, and to consent to the onward journey, even though it inevitably leads into a 'cloud of unknowing'.

What guiding wisdom can help us as we move beyond the horizon of all that we know? First we may need to be encouraged to leave the safety of our comfort zones. Overcoming the natural human tendency to stay with what is safe and familiar is a huge step, and often it is something we only do when circumstances lead us into a cleft 'between a rock and a hard place'. With hindsight, however, we may realize that this was a moment of real inner growth and the touch of grace.

> Deep in the sea are riches beyond compare,
> But if you seek safety, it is on the shore.
> **Saadi of Shiraz**[24]

The greatest hindrance to this ongoing journey is the illusion of certainty. As human beings living in a world where nothing is fully predictable and nothing is ultimately in our own control, there can be no 'absolute truth' as defined by the human mind. The 'absolute truth' we long for, however, can be discovered in moments when we absolutely know the touch of God in the core of our being. This is a *heart-knowing*. It flows from our deepest levels of experience, and we can *trust* that experience in a way that we can never fully trust the formulations of the human mind. The mind can very

---

There is no hidden poet in me, just a little piece of God that might grow into poetry.
Etty Hillesum

easily get things wrong, but the heart, at its deepest level, runs true.

For so many people agnosticism sits very uneasily with faith. Faith, they think, means being certain of your beliefs... But is this what faith really is? It might rather be that faith is a sort of insight into the nature of reality, an insight which does not increase ordinary factual knowledge, but sets all our knowledge and experience in a new perspective... True faith might actually decrease our 'religious' certainties, as we realize how little we know or can say about God and how much depends on the wordless experience that all religious doctrines only dimly and inadequately point towards.
Keith Ward[25]

Wisdom consists of being comfortable with certainty and uncertainty... Strangely, wisdom often arrives only after thinking is over. Instead of turning a situation over from every angle, one arrives at a point where simplicity dawns. In the presence of a wise person one can feel an interior calm, alive and breathing its own atmosphere, that needs no outside validation. The ups and downs of existence are all one. The New Testament calls this 'the peace that passes understanding', because it goes beyond thinking.
Deepak Chopra[26]

The truth of the heart lies deeper than intellectual

Whoever opts for revenge digs two graves.
Chinese proverb

certainty, and sometimes we may have to let go of our lesser 'certainties' in order to allow the truth to flow with power. Christians would see this flow as the power of the Holy Spirit, an energy that is always seeking to bring life from whatever we present, and which always flows free, emerging where we least expect it, and sometimes blocked by our efforts to channel it where we think it should be going.

> *The Kingdom is not an institution but God's vision for the whole of humanity living within the consciousness of God's all-pervading presence...*
>
> *Only the open-minded are truly able to read the 'signs of the times', because the Spirit blows where She wills, and in some surprising directions. Being open means being continually a searcher. A searcher with an open mind finds that the right person, the right word, the right experience, the right book enters our life at just the moment needed for us to learn the next lesson, to take the next step. 'When the pupil is ready, the teacher appears.' If we are not open and observant, that moment will be lost, maybe never to be repeated.*
>
> **Adrian B. Smith**[27]

Yet, ironically, our own experience of God can also be a block on our onward journeying. We so cherish our 'mountain-top experiences', and we can resist journeying on to the range of unclimbed peaks that still lie ahead of us.

God is always bigger than the boxes we build for God, so do not waste too much time protecting the boxes.
Richard Rohr

The last experience of God is frequently the greatest obstacle to the next experience of God. We make an absolute out of it and use it to strengthen our ego, to self-aggrandize and self-congratulate. Then, of course, nothing more happens.
Richard Rohr[28]

The unknown author of the following piece of wisdom seeks to assure us that wherever we journey, into whatever unknown territory that lies ahead, God precedes us and accompanies us:

Our highest truths are but half-truths.
Think not to settle down for ever in any truth.
Make use of it, as a tent to pass a summer's night,
But build no house on it, or it will be your tomb.
When you first have an inkling of its insufficiency,
And begin to descry a dim counter-truth looming up beyond,
Then weep not, but give thanks; it is the Lord whispering,
'Take up thy bed, and walk.'
Arthur James[29]

On letting go

One of life's ironies is that for new life to emerge there always has to be a letting-go. The trees have to let go of their leaves just when they are at their most radiant. Birth is only possible when the safe space of the womb is relinquished. Letting go is one of the hardest of life's

---

The God of any religion is only a fragment of God.
Deepak Chopra

challenges. Sacred scripture is full of examples of people who had to let go of what seemed good and final, in order to journey towards something more. 'The good' it is sometimes said 'is often the enemy of the better.'

In his poem 'Walking Away', C. Day Lewis describes the pain of letting go that he has experienced with his growing son, beginning with the boy's first football game at school, eighteen years earlier. More serious and final partings will follow, but the memory of this one never leaves him, but instead guides him to the wisdom that the final test of our love for someone is our willingness to let them go.

> *I have had worse partings, but none that so*
> *Gnaws at my mind still. Perhaps it is roughly*
> *Saying what God alone could perfectly show -*
> *How selfhood begins with a walking away*
> *And love is proved in the letting go.*
> **C. Day Lewis**[30]

The cost of holding on to what we long to cling to is high. As Henri Nouwen warns us:

What you cling to ends up rotting in your hands.
Henri Nouwen[31]

This theme is expanded by Rabindranath Tagore, who warns us that if we try to hold on to something we cherish, we can actually crush the life out of it.

When we are ready to die at any moment,
we are also ready to live at any moment.
Henri Nouwen

Why did the lamp go out?
I smothered it with my coat,
To protect it from the storm.
That's why the lamp went out.

Why die the flower fade?
I pressed it to my heart
In fear-filled love.
That's why the flower faded.

Why did the river dry up?
I built a dam
To keep it all for myself.
That's why the river dried up.
Why did the harp-string snap?
I wanted to force a note from it
That it could not give.
That's why the harp-string snapped.
Rabindranath Tagore[32]

We don't have to let the lamp go out. Nor need the flower fade or the river dry up. In everything we have the choice, to cling to what is past or to allow the future to unfold, to share the gifts of God with all creation, or to keep them locked up for ourselves. Each one of us has the choice, moment by moment, to leave the world a better, or a worse place, for our having lived here.

Nothing is more dangerous than people who presume they already see. God can most easily be lost by being thought found.
Richard Rohr

When you appeared in this world you cried, and all the people around you rejoiced. Live your life in such a way that when you leave this world you will rejoice, and all the people around you will cry.
Indian wisdom

Christianity is about learning to inhabit the square foot on which one stands.
Monica Furlong

Life Wisdom

When I was a little girl, I sometimes heard the comment that
a particular person in my family or circle of acquaintances
had been educated in 'the university of life'. In my early years
I often wondered about this remarkable establishment that
engendered such wisdom in its graduates. Perhaps I even
wondered whether I would ever gain admission to such a
centre of learning. I needn't have worried. We are all enrolled,
whether we like it or not. But whether we actually learn
anything there is up to us, of course.

When I reflect on what wisdom means, and where it
comes from, I am coming to the conclusion that wisdom
is not a product of learning, but the fruit of experience.
Experience alone, however, is not sufficient to produce the
fruit. The experience needs to be reflected upon if it is to
ripen into wisdom. Life supplies us all with a constant
supply of experience. The challenge is to reflect on that
experience and allow it to distil into wisdom. In this section
we will explore some of the forms this life-experience may
take and what fruits it may yield.

Wisdom is seeing the extra-ordinary in the ordinary.
John Martin Sahajananda

As we embark on this exploration, we might begin by joining the Irish poet-philosopher Patrick Kavanagh, perched perhaps in his favourite spot on the banks of the Liffey, as he muses:

> *And I have a feeling*
> *That through the hole in reason's ceiling*
> *We can fly to knowledge*
> *Without ever going to college.*
>
> **Patrick Kavanagh**[1]

The gift of experience

When you awoke this morning, you had absolutely no idea of what the new day would bring. You may have had your schedule for the day, your definite agenda, your 'to-do list', but quite probably when evening falls, you will remember not so much the things you meant to do, but the surprises that came in sideways, that delighted or derailed you. While the routine chores of living run on relentlessly along our carefully prepared and well-oiled tracks, the moments that interrupt this smooth line of operations are what Kavanagh calls 'the holes in reason's ceiling'. We might well wish we could avoid them. They make life unpredictable and even hazardous, because we can't prepare our response to them. They demand our spontaneity, and that can make us feel very vulnerable. Emily Dickinson compares this process of fielding life's surprises to the action of walking across a rickety bridge.

We are strangers and sojourners, soft dots on the rocks.
Annie Dillard

> *I stepped from plank to plank*
> *So slow and cautiously;*
> *The stars about my head I felt,*
> *About my feet the sea.*

> *I knew not but the next*
> *Would be my final inch –*
> *This gave me that precarious gait*
> *Some call experience.*
> **Emily Dickinson[2]**

Yet these unplanned intrusions can also be the catalysts that make us grow, and so the first requirement is to be open to them. Sometimes this opening is both risky and costly. Sometimes we fail to be open because we simply don't believe that there is more to ourselves, and each other, and life, than what we can see. What matters is to be aware of the mystery that life conceals, and to let our choices reflect what really leads to fuller and more meaningful living:

> *I realized it for the first time in my life: there is nothing but mystery in the world, how it hides behind the fabric of our poor, browbeat days, shining brightly, and we don't even know it.*
> *'You know, some things don't matter that much, Lily. Like the colour of a house. How big is that in the overall scheme of life? But lifting a person's heart – now, that matters. The whole problem with people is…'*

A man can see further through a tear than a telescope.
Bruce Lee

'They don't know what matters and what doesn't,' I said,
filling in her sentence and feeling proud of myself for doing so.
'I was gonna say, The problem is they know what
matters, but they don't choose it… the hardest thing on
earth is choosing what matters.'
Sue Monk Kidd[3]

Bruce Lee, too, finds the spiritual in the everyday and urges us to be open to it, and to trust our experience:

Let the spiritual, unbidden and unconscious, grow up
through the common.
Bruce Lee[4]

Such awareness of the hidden mystery of things is the gift of insight – the harvest that grows when both eyes and heart are open:

Mere sight is what we see; insight is how we see it. Mere
sight can only behold; it takes insight to comprehend. Both
the eyes and the heart must be open.
Robert Kirschner[5]

So how do we reflect on our experience in such a way as to uncover its wisdom? Sometimes I think of 'prayer' as a little bit like beach-combing. We walk the shoreline of life day by day, and sometimes the experience will catch our attention and demand to be noticed, like some beautiful

---

Whatever else one may know, one does not know God.
Meister Eckhart

shell that startles us with a reflection of how beautiful our own souls can be, or a piece of wreckage that refuses to let us forget how broken we are. The daily journey of life brings its own nuggets of wisdom. All we need are eyes to notice and a heart to gather the harvest that today's incoming tide has deposited in our memory. Mary Wainwright has some guidance to offer:

Sing your experience as a verse, part of the song sung
by the soul of the world.
Examine every day of your life to find its meaning,
however small that may seem.
Listen to the earth as she breathes, to the universal pulse that
runs through all our lives.
Remember with humility our connection to each other
and to the divine.
Surrender to the guiding hand, which we may not see,
but that touches us all.
Have courage to show your light through the mists
of earthly confusion.
Dance to the rhythms you thought you had forgotten.
Bring truth to each day.

Find joy in your being.
Be still, be silent, be aware, be peace
And you will know the reason for your existence.
Mary Wainwright[6]

Patience is not passive, on the contrary
it is concentrated strength.
Bruce Lee

When our small daughter was learning to use crayons and pencils, she came to me one day with a sheet of what can only be called 'scribble'. I admired it with a mother's eyes, told her how fine it was, and then (silly me!) asked her what it meant. She gave me one of those disdainful looks that only a toddler can produce, and responded: 'I don't know what it means. I only "wrot" it!'

I often think back to that sentence, and wonder whether I should include it in the preface of any book I write myself! However, I had to smile when I discovered that far greater beings than I have the same problem in knowing what they mean, and prefer simply to live their meanings, and let significance evolve in the living.

> *There is a story of a Russian ballerina who gave a superbly moving performance at the Kirov Ballet, leaving the audience enraptured at what they knew to be a uniquely inspired occasion. Afterwards, she was asked, 'And what did it mean?'*
> *'What did it mean?', she responded, 'What did it mean? If I could say what it meant, I would not have danced it.'*
> **Keith Ward**[7]

Mitch Albom even thinks heaven exists to enable us to make sense of ourselves:

> *That's what heaven is. You get to make sense of your yesterdays.*
> **Mitch Albom**[8]

To live is to change; to be perfect is to have changed often.
John Henry Newman

The greatness in the least of us
Stephen Hawking, one who quite literally reaches for the stars, reminds us that:

We are very small,
but we are profoundly capable
of very big things.

Where does this greatness come from? For the medieval German mystic, Meister Eckhart, the greatness of which each of us is capable, is the fruit of a seed of divinity itself within us:

The seed of God exists in us. Given a hard worker and a good director it thrives apace and grows up into God whose seed it is, and its fruit is likewise God's nature. Pear seed grows up into pear tree, nut seed grows up into nut tree – God seed into God, to God.

This call to greatness is not limited to those whom the world recognizes as great historic personalities. It is something that each of us can and must embrace:

Just as once it was Pavel's time in Hungary and Mandela's time in South Africa and Mary Robinson's time in Ireland – all simple people who emerged against impossible odds – it is my time right here, in this tiny city right now. What happens here now is my responsibility. What happens

---

The unexamined life is not worth living.
Socrates

tomorrow is my legacy to it. It is not a matter of doing great things. No, it is far worse than that. It is a matter of doing small things courageously.
Joan Chittister[9]

To become fully human is to live in such a way that this hidden greatness can flourish, and lead to the greater good of all creation. The greatness that we carry is ours to choose, if we dare, but so too are the fears that hold us back, not least the great fear that we could be more, much more, than we allow ourselves to be:

The ideal is hidden inside you, and the obstacle to reaching this ideal is also inside you. You have to hand all the material you need to create this ideal.
Leo Tolstoy[10]

It's OK to be *you*!

The journey from the crying baby over whom the world rejoices, to the dying man or woman, over whose death the world grieves is a long road indeed, and so often we spend much of it trying to be someone else. We believe, perhaps, that 'who we are' is just not good enough, and maybe this negative message has been reinforced by family, school, or church. Or we believe that we have to prove ourselves in some way, and that everyone else on earth is living better than we are.

It is not the place we occupy which is important but the direction in which we move.
Oliver Wendell Holmes

A truly wise teacher never tries to impose a wisdom from outside ourselves, but to draw out the wisdom that is within us:

> *The teacher who walks in the shadow of the temple, among his followers, gives not of his wisdom but rather of his faith and his lovingness.*
>
> *If he is indeed wise he does not bid you enter the house of his wisdom, but rather leads you to the threshold of your own mind.*
>
> **Kahlil Gibran**[11]

What a shame that the little boy in the following story didn't have a teacher like that. Perhaps his experience touches on your own memories:

> *He always wanted to say things, but no one understood.*
>
> *He always wanted to explain things. But no one cared.*
> *So he drew.*
>
> *Sometimes he would just draw and it wasn't anything.*
> *He wanted to carve it in stone or write it in the sky.*
>
> *He would lie out on the grass and look up in the sky and it would be only him and the sky and the things inside that needed saying.*
>
> *And it was after that, that he drew the picture. It was a beautiful picture. He kept it under the pillow and would let no one see it.*
>
> *And he would look at it every night and think about it. And*

To be dead is to stop believing in the masterpieces we will begin tomorrow.
Patrick Kavanagh

when it was dark, and his eyes were closed, he could still see it.

And it was all of him. And he loved it.

When he started school he brought it with him. Not to show anyone, but just to have it with him like a friend.

It was funny about school.

He sat in a square, brown desk like all the other brown desks, and he thought it should be red.

And his room was a square, brown room. Like all the other rooms.

And it was tight and close. And stiff.

He hated to hold his pencil and the chalk, with his arm stiff and his feet flat on the floor, with the teacher watching and watching.

And then he had to write numbers. And they weren't anything.

They were worse than the letters that could be something if you put them together.

And the numbers were tight and square and he hated the whole thing.

The teacher came and spoke to him. She told him to wear a tie like all the other boys. He said he didn't like them and she said it didn't matter.

After that they drew. And he drew all yellow and it was the way he felt about morning. And it was beautiful.

The teacher came and smiled at him. 'What's this?' she said. 'Why don't you draw something like Ken's drawing? Isn't it beautiful?'

It was all questions.

Anyone who thinks that politics and religion don't mix is not reading the same Bible I am.
Desmond Tutu

After that his mother bought him a tie and he always drew airplanes and rocket ships like everyone else.

And when he lay out alone looking at the sky, it was big and blue and all of everything, but he wasn't any more.

He was square inside and brown, and his hands were stiff, and he was like anyone else. And the thing inside him that needed saying didn't need saying any more.

It had stopped pushing. It was crushed. Stiff. Like everything else.

Peter Lomas[12]

I was once visiting a 'living museum' where there was a reconstructed Victorian schoolhouse, where visitors could experience the rigours of a Victorian schoolday.

The schoolroom was full, with both adults and children. The 'teacher' told us to copy a drawing of a bridge that he had pinned up on the blackboard. Everyone duly did as instructed. Forty or so identical bridges appeared on forty or so ancient slates, and the teacher prowled round the class, cane in hand, to check our handiwork. Suddenly he alighted on one hapless 'student'.

'What's that?' he stormed, glowering at the pupil's slate.

'It's a d...d...uck,' the unfortunate scholar replied.

'Did I tell you to draw a *duck* under the bridge?' roared the teacher.

'I just thought it would look nice,' the pupil muttered.

Love for God; love for neighbour. These are two sides of the same coin. The true chapel of the heart embraces both.
Desmond Tutu

'You're not here to *think*...' came the reply!

And let us not forget that we can suffocate each other with disabling kindness as surely as we can stab each other with harsh criticism. There is no end to the ways in which we can give out the signal that 'it isn't OK to be you'. I hope that nothing will deter you from drawing as many ducks as you wish under the bridges of your life. I hope nothing will be allowed to block *your* freedom to be *you*.

The power of love...

Rainforests have fallen in the cause of the human need to express our feelings about love. Love, we might well think, makes fools of us all, so what has love to do with wisdom?

Louis de Bernières describes as a 'temporary madness' the human experience of falling in love:

Love is a temporary madness; it erupts like volcanoes and then it subsides. And when it subsides you have to make a decision. You have to work out whether your roots have become so entwined together that it is inconceivable that you should ever part. Because this is what love is. Love is not breathlessness, it is not excitement... No... that is just being in love, which any fool can do. Love itself is what is left over when being in love has burned away.
Louis de Bernières[13]

Happiness and unhappiness are simply the high and low tides on the edge of a great sea called contentment.
Source unknown

And Michael Mayne warns us that:

The opposite of love is not hate, but indifference, the failure to care – or to care enough. It is a want of imagination, a lack of empathy, an inability or a refusal to see in another human being a creature as frail and as easily hurt as I can be.
Michael Mayne[14]

To move from 'being in love' to 'loving' is a real challenge. It demands effort, care and commitment, and a substantial surrendering of personal freedom. Those who fail to make this transition are in real danger of passing from one 'temporary madness' to the next, without ever actually experiencing love. To live from a central core of love, an attitude of heart that habitually places 'other' before 'self', will yield a power of spirit that will overflow into everything we do, and will ultimately affect all creation positively:

And what is it to work with love?
 It is to weave the cloth with threads drawn from your heart, even as if your beloved were to wear that cloth.
 It is to build a house with affection, even as if your beloved were to dwell in that house.
 It is to sow seeds with tenderness and reap the harvest with joy, even as if your beloved were to eat the fruit.
 It is to charge all things you fashion with a breath of your own spirit.
Kahlil Gibran[15]

Ideals are like the stars; we never reach them, but like the mariners of the sea, we chart our course by them.
Carl Schurz

After the world-shaking events of 11 September 2001, words from Thornton Wilder were used to express something of the condolence the world then felt with the people who had been personally affected by the terrorist attack on the Twin Towers in New York:

Soon we shall die... we shall be loved for a while and forgotten. But the love will have been enough; all those impulses of love return to the love that made them. Even memory is not necessary for love. There is a land of the living and a land of the dead, and the bridge is love, the only survival, the only meaning.
Thornton Wilder[16]

And it was true. The devastation in Manhattan did indeed release a spirit of genuine loving and caring that surprised the world in general, and New Yorkers in particular. In the ruins of our hopes we sometimes discover the seeds of our highest dreams. In the aftermath of any catastrophe, there is often an outpouring of heroism, of solidarity, of compassion and of generosity. Heart reaches out to heart, and human beings can grow a notch closer to the fullness of our humanity. Brian Keenan, held hostage in Lebanon, describes the deep bonding that evolved between those who found themselves randomly thrust together in the depths of a nightmare situation, and he notices the parallel with Wilder's novel, *The Bridge of San Luis Rey*, which tells how a bridge collapsed, carrying five people with it into the chasm below.

Watch for the big problems. They disguise big opportunities.
Source unknown

The men I watched silently, or talked and argued with, these men with whom I laughed and played, were for me the five people on that bridge over the St Luis Rey. We each of us had fallen down into meaning, if we cared to seek it out, and to climb with it out of that awful chasm into which we had been toppled. The experience of love was the stepladder up which we could climb.
Brian Keenan[17]

Perhaps something of the secret of love is to be found in these two experiences: when we face the worst, the only route to travel beyond it is in *relationship*. Relationship is the key to the whole human venture. We become truly ourselves, when we are able to be truly in relationship with each other. The wisdom of love lies, perhaps, in the discovery that love is very much more than romance; love is about embracing our interrelatedness, and living from this deeper centre.

Relationship is a process of self-revelation. Relationship is the mirror in which you discover yourself – to be is to be related.
Bruce Lee[18]

Despite the appearance of disparity, we are all of us bound together in one design. Beyond the boundaries that appear to divide us is a divine gravity that holds us fast.
Robert Kirschner[19]

Injustice anywhere is a threat to justice everywhere.
Martin Luther King Jr

In the aftermath of the London bombings of 7 July 2005, this sense of bonding was even apparent on the Internet. In the need to be in communication, and indeed in conversation with others, many people posted messages and on-scene photographs of these terrible events on the Web. This was a reaching-out of human to human with the message: 'We are all linked into this, and we are with you.'

The inward journey, if followed with commitment and courage, leads us through and beyond our subjective lives, because the spirit 'within' us is the same spirit that is found in everything else. To encounter the spirit within the psyche is to encounter a reality that longs for involvement with others, and this spirit is not truly satisfied unless it has found communion with the world and exchange with other people...

Genuine spiritual awakening is always followed by a centrifugal movement away from self towards the world and the transcendent. In our typical human experience, God starts off as 'my' God, my personal redeemer, guiding angel or mentor, and ends up as the supreme and unknowable Godhead, the great mystery who is creator of the world and the reality within every thing.

David Tacey[20]

This 'centrifugal movement away from self' can have dramatic results – world-changing results.

Pamela Hussey, writing about the courage of ordinary

Experience is not what happens to you; it is what you do with what happens to you.
Aldous Huxley

women in El Salvador under a vicious dictatorship records 'Susan's story':

> In answer to the question 'Who is my neighbour?' put to him by a teacher of the Law, Jesus told the story of the Good Samaritan (Luke 10:30–37). Susan told me this story:
>
> A woman we work with came in one morning: the bus had been stopped at a checkpoint, the woman beside her didn't have up-to-date papers and the soldiers started giving her a hard time. She explained that because so many of the mayors' offices had been burnt down she hadn't been able to get her papers. So the soldier said, 'Well, what were you doing in that area – there were guerrillas there last night – you must have been helping them.' Then he looked round and asked, 'Can anyone vouch for this woman and confirm that what she is saying is true?' The woman who works for us said, 'Yes, I can vouch for her – I can guarantee that it's true.' She had never seen the woman in her life, but to me it's an example of the kingdom of God. At that moment that woman did become her friend: she saw a person in need and she responded, and she wasn't lying when she said 'This woman's my friend.' And the soldier let the other woman go. That is Christian living at its most basic. These women have found the spirit of liberation. People like that, who can't be controlled by fear, are liberated.
>
> **Pamela Hussey**[21]

The quieter you become the more you can hear.
Baba Ram Dass

When the power of love releases us from our self-focus, we recognize that all men and women are indeed our brothers and sisters. It then becomes impossible to ignore their pain or their need. Labels of race or creed or social status lose all credibility when seen through the lens of authentic loving.

Love brings responsibility in its wake – a responsibility which we embrace gladly for the sake of the beloved, and personal love is always a sacrament – a sign of what *could* be, of something much larger, of something universal. We find such a sign in the little prince's 'taming' of his solitary rose:

And he went back to meet the fox.

'Goodbye,' he said.

'Goodbye,' said the fox. 'And now here is my secret, a very simple secret: It is only with the heart that one can see rightly; what is essential is invisible to the eye.'

'What is essential is invisible to the eye,' the little prince repeated, so that he would be sure to remember.

'It is the time you have wasted for your rose that makes your rose so important.'

'It is the time I have wasted for my rose' – said the little prince, so that he would be sure to remember.

'Men have forgotten this truth,' said the fox. 'But you must not forget it. You become responsible, forever, for whatever you have tamed. You are responsible for your rose…'

The road to success is under construction.
Source unknown

'I am responsible for my rose,' the little prince repeated, so that he would be sure to remember.
Antoine de Saint-Exupéry[22]

Prayer has sometimes been described as 'wasting time with God'. To 'waste time' with the beloved is the way we grow the bonds that connect us to the heart of each other. Just as the child's experiences cause new neural connections to be formed in the maturing brain, until the fully developed mind emerges, so too we learn to grow our 'heart-links' until a fully developed humanity emerges. The little prince and his rose are an image of this truth.

The secret of heaven: that each affects the other and the other affects the next, and the world is full of stories, but the stories are all one.
Mitch Albom[23]

… and the tyranny of fear

Love has one great enemy. Love's enemy is fear. Fear holds us back from the best that we could be – fear of what others may think of us or do to us. Fear of losing our security or our status. Or quite simply fear of the unknown, that keeps us locked inside prisons of our own making.

Never doubt the power of a small group of committed people to change the world.

Life is so beautiful that death has fallen in love with it, a jealous possessive love that grabs at what it can. But life leaps over oblivion lightly, losing only a thing or two of no importance, and gloom is but the passing shadow of a cloud.

I must say a word about fear. It is life's only true opponent. Only fear can defeat life. It is a clever, treacherous adversary, how well I know it. It has no decency, respects no law or convention, shows no mercy. It goes for your weakest spot, which it finds with unerring ease. It begins in your mind, always... Fear next turns to your body, which is already aware that something terribly wrong is going on... Quickly you make rash decisions. You dismiss your last allies: hope and trust. There, you've defeated yourself. Fear, which is but an impression, has triumphed in you.

Yann Martell[24]

Fear turns us into cowards and colluders, unable or unwilling to respond as human beings to the needs of others, or to speak out against injustice:

> *They persecuted the black people.*
> *I wasn't black, and I said nothing.*
>
> *Then they persecuted the Native Americans.*
> *I wasn't a Native American, and I said nothing.*

That's the only way it has ever happened in the past.
Margaret Mead

Then they persecuted the Jews.
I wasn't a Jew, and I said nothing.

Then they persecuted the asylum seekers.
I wasn't an asylum seeker, and I said nothing.

Finally they turned on me.
But there was no one left, to say anything.
Source unknown

Fear also makes us pin everything down, hold it in a tight grip, try to control it at all costs. Afraid of each other, we hold back from full relationship. Afraid of creation itself, we try to subjugate it. Our defence systems are formidable, but they are rendered powerless when confronted by the Love that loosens nails:

And then came man, with his hammer and his bag of nails.
And he nailed the shining sun to the heavens,
in case it should leave him cold.
And he nailed the bright moon fast to the silent sky,
for fear of being left in darkness.
And he nailed the clouds to the shifting wind
so they would not gather above him.
And he nailed down the salt sea and each fish fast within it.
And he nailed the bright birds to the empty air,
And every creature that flew, or walked, or crawled, or slithered,
he nailed hard in its allotted place.

Never deprive someone of hope; it might be all they have.
H. Jackson Brown Jr

And then came a carpenter's son.
And man, afraid, took him and nailed him tight to a tree,
For this man's tongue could loosen nails.
John Ballard[25]

Fear has one good fruit, however. It can call forth a response of true courage. In her novel *To Kill a Mockingbird*, Harper Lee gives us a fine example of human courage in the face of injustice, discrimination and persecution. Here Atticus, a lawyer of great integrity, who has put his reputation, and his own and his family's safety on the line in defence of a victimized black labourer, speaks to his son Jem about courage:

I wanted you to see what real courage is, instead of getting the idea that courage is a man with a gun in his hand. It's when you know you're licked before you begin but you begin anyway and you see it through no matter what. You rarely win, but sometimes you do.
  The one thing that doesn't abide by majority rule is a person's conscience.
Harper Lee[26]

Atticus knows how it feels to swim against the tide, but he also knows that sometimes, perhaps most times, the tide is flowing in the wrong direction.

If only I may grow firmer, simpler, quieter, warmer.
Dag Hammarskjöld

Embracing change

Very few people welcome change in their lives. We all began
our existence in the comfort zone of our mother's womb.
When we were forced out of it, we probably cried, with all
the power of our still undeveloped lungs. And since then,
whenever we are forced out of a comfort zone we squeal
inwardly, and if we have the chance, we build up our
defences, to protect the safe place we are inhabiting.

And yet the spiritual journey challenges us constantly to
let go of our securities and leave our current comfort zone.
In the faith story of the Judaeo-Christian tradition, we
discover this pattern repeatedly – from Abraham and
Moses, through the wanderings of the children of Israel
in the wilderness, in search of the Promised Land, to the
warning of the risen Christ to Mary Magdalene: 'Don't
cling!'

In the words of André Gide:

*One does not discover new lands without consenting to lose
sight of the shore.*

Those 'new lands' take many forms. From where we are
standing today we cannot even guess at what tomorrow's
terrain may look like. There is only one way to find out, and
that is to step out fearlessly, leaving the past behind, with
gratitude for all that it has brought us and taught us, and
risking tomorrow in the trust that it too will one day
become a cherished 'yesterday'.

A smooth sea never made a skilful mariner.
English proverb

Life is moving, evolving. There are things that we cannot do today because of our limitations, our youth, our fears. But tomorrow, or with time, new strengths will grow up in us. We are in the process of changing; others are changing too. We must know how to wait patiently. We must know how to befriend time.

In Chinese, the word 'crisis' implies danger, but also opportunity. Crises may bring a threat of death, but they are also the opportunity for a new start in life, a rebirth. In Greek, the word implies the need to move forward, to make a choice in order to escape from a situation in which we have become trapped.

Jean Vanier[27]

Our journey of life, our journeys of love and our journey of faith, are all journeys into the unknown. None of them offers us a 'safe' passage, let alone a safe harbour. There is a great danger of stagnation if we settle in our certainties, especially in the imagined 'certainties' of faith. Helder Camara warns us to avoid such stagnation at all costs:

*Pilgrim
when your ship
long moored in harbour
gives you the illusion
of being a house;
when your ship begins to put down roots
in the stagnant water by the quay*

To a mind that is still the whole universe surrenders.
Chuang Tzu

PUT OUT TO SEA!
Save your boat's journeying soul
And your own pilgrim soul,
Cost what it may!
Helder Camara[28]

Say not, 'I have found the truth,' but rather 'I have found
a truth.'
Say not, 'I have found the path of the soul.' Say rather,
'I have met the soul walking upon my path.'
For the soul walks on all paths.
The soul walks not upon a line, neither does it grow like
a reed.
The soul unfolds itself, like a lotus of countless petals.
Kahlil Gibran[29]

Faith is not a conquered peak but a daunting ascent; not a
safe harbour but a long voyage. No one hands faith to us.
There are only hands to hold as we search for it together.
Robert Kirschner[30]

We must never assume that we possess the truth. Truth
must posses us. Truth is infinite. 'I am Truth,' says Jesus.
We enter into Truth by losing ourselves in the Mystery that
is beyond our capacity. It is exposure to Truth that brings us
to holiness.
Ruth Burrows[31]

What is a cynic? A man who knows the price of everything
and the value of nothing.
Oscar Wilde

Sometimes life's wisdom emerges at the most vulnerable moments, when life itself is at risk, or even extinguished. This is the prayer used at the funeral of a girl of eighteen who was killed in a road accident. When all has been surrendered, a nugget of eternity is revealed, and this prayer expresses in just a few words the very essence of what it means to be alive, to be growing, and to be human. It is a fitting close to our brief excursion into the limitless realm of 'life wisdom'.

> *Think deeply*
> *Speak gently*
> *Love much*
> *Laugh often*
> *Work hard*
> *Give freely*
> *Pray earnestly*
> *And be kind.*
> **Source unknown**

People may doubt what you say,
but they will believe what you do.
Source unknown

Unfolding Wisdom

As I sit here at my desk, my hands on the keyboard of my computer, and my eyes focused on the view from the window, I find myself wondering what people perhaps ten thousand years from now will make of how we human beings are today. I think I am using state-of-the-art technology to write about the deep wisdom of life, and if I am honest I would have to admit that I am vaguely assuming that as a member of the human race, I am part of the 'finished product'. Yet my reason and my intuition both challenge these certainties! Ten thousand years from now people (if there are any left) may be examining the fossils of Homo sapiens and concluding that, though certainly human, we were really very primitive.

It's a humbling thought, but it is also an encouraging one, because it would mean that life's story is still not yet fully told, and that God's creative work continues through the course of change and growth that we call evolution. It would be a reminder that we are not yet ready to receive the mystery of God in all its fullness, but that we are certainly on the way. The stories revealed in the spiritual

---

Creativity flourishes not in certainty but in questions.
Sue Monk Kidd

traditions of humankind reveal how this story has been unfolding through history. We have every reason to trust that it will continue to unfold.

So where are we now?

Life's unfinished story

Many voices are suggesting that we are in fact on the threshold of a whole new form of consciousness – one that we find extraordinarily difficult either to understand or to articulate. These prophetic voices are intimating that the human family as a whole is growing in reflective self-awareness, growing in a sense of how intimately all life forms are interrelated and interdependent, growing more and more towards the fullness of our humanity.

> *At one time, conscious self-awareness was alive in only a fraction of the existing humans. But the destiny of the species was forever altered when this form of consciousness emerged in increasing numbers until in time it became the determining characteristic of humanity. So too with us. A new form of consciousness is beginning to emerge in a small slice of contemporary Homo sapiens. As with the early self-aware primates, we are astounded by the new awareness and when we go to speak of it, we discover that we have no easy or established or efficient way of transmitting this mode of consciousness.*
> **Brian Swimme**[1]

**We cannot live the afternoon of life according to
the programme of life's morning.**
C.G. Jung

Personally I can look back over only half a century of this growing consciousness, but what I see convinces me that we are indeed in an accelerating process of change and growth. Fifty years ago, few people would have questioned the legitimacy of war as a means of resolving disputes. Today, millions protest against the use of military force. Fifty years ago, only a small minority of ecology enthusiasts were concerned with the well-being of the planet. Today it is unacceptable *not* to be environmentally aware. Fifty years ago, social, gender and economic inequality and injustice were considered to be 'the way things are'. Today we rightly struggle for justice, especially on behalf of the weak and marginalized, and the poorest countries in our world. So, yes, I believe we *are* moving forwards, in spite of a great deal of evidence to the contrary.

> *Nothing is more wrong than to treat the human as though it has been biologically stationary since the ending of the Ice Age. It may be that to macroscopic observation nothing has changed during this period in the generalised arrangement of the cerebral neurons. But on the other hand, what an extraordinary and irreversible increase of collective consciousness is manifest in the appearance, association and opposition of techniques, visions, passions and ideas! What an intensification of reflective life!*
> **Teilhard de Chardin**[2]

The Christian vision sees the incarnation of Jesus of

Nothing is as apt to mask the face of God as religion.
Martin Buber

Nazareth as the pivotal event in this radical change in human consciousness. Two thousand years ago, a human being was born who not only embodied the divine consciousness in himself, but, through his Spirit, empowered the human family to discover the core of our being in God. This transforming moment in human history invites us to enter into realms of wisdom that our minds cannot either understand or express.

> *The great conviction of the New Testament is that Jesus by giving us His Spirit has dramatically transformed the fabric of human consciousness. Our redemption by Jesus Christ has opened up for us levels of consciousness that can be described by St Paul only in terms of a totally new creation...*
>
> *The all-important aim in Christian meditation is to allow God's mysterious and silent presence within us to become more and more not only a reality, but the reality in our lives; to let it become that reality which gives meaning, shape and purpose to everything we do, to everything we are.*
> **John Main**[3]

There are many who see a new reflection of this defining moment of grace in our contemporary experience of change and transition. We may feel that we are floundering in a collective chaos, in which old certainties have been lost and new ways ahead are still just experimental, but such a chaos

---

There is no place so awake and alive as the edge of becoming.
Sue Monk Kidd

can also be a place of potential for new growth. It can become a space for transformation.

> *As we enter the twenty-first century, we are experiencing a moment of grace. Such moments are privileged moments. The great transformations of the universe occur at such times...*
>
> *There are cosmological and historical moments of grace as well as religious moments of grace. The present is one of those moments that can be considered as a cosmological, as well as a historical and a religious moment of grace... Something new is happening. A new vision and a new energy are coming into being... A comprehensive change of consciousness is coming over the human community.*
> **Thomas Berry**[4]

If this is true, then we can believe that this growth in consciousness is indeed drawing us closer to God, and to the ground of our being, and that it is directed and guided by the Holy Spirit.

> *It is the inner movement of the Spirit, immanent in nature, which brings about the evolution of matter and life into human consciousness, and the same Spirit at work in human consciousness, latent in every man, is always at work leading to divine life.*
> **Bede Griffiths**[5]

**The road behind us becomes what freed us
for the road ahead.**
Joan Chittister

Teilhard de Chardin re-echoes this conviction, and sees it as a promise of unimaginable possibilities to come:

The day will come when, after harnessing the ether, the winds, the tides, gravitation, we shall harness for God the energies of love. And, on that day, for the second time in the history of the world, human beings will have discovered fire.
Teilhard de Chardin[6]

Perhaps that day is already at hand. Perhaps it began to dawn two thousand years ago, and, even as we watch, a new sun is rising, whose light will both shame and enlighten us:

The time is right for a type of religious quantum leap – not into some vast unknown, but into the deep story, the well-spring of spiritual awakening which existed before, and will continue to flourish long after, every religion known to humankind will have faded into history.
Diairmuid Ó'Murchú[7]

Science and spirituality – a new-found friendship
One of the most encouraging trends of our times is the growing convergence between different ways of looking at life. Global communications have opened up all our hearts and minds to the fact that there are many different ways of

---

The truth may set you free, but first it will shatter the safe, sweet way you live.
Sue Monk Kidd

responding to the challenge of being human on planet earth, and widespread travel has stretched our experience even as it has shrunk the globe we inhabit.

One particular line of convergence is that between science and spirituality. Until very recently, science and religion have often been seen as antagonists. Science pursues the truth about the material world and relies on observation, experiment and analysis. On the face of it there can be little hope of dialogue with religion and spirituality, which probe the power and the mystery of a world that is unseen, not amenable to conventional observation, and can only be approached through intuitive channels. Science, traditionally, is deeply distrustful of intuition, and religion is not content to stay merely with that which can be observed. For centuries, the two have agreed to differ, and for many lay people, not versed in either discipline, it seemed one had to decide whether to trust science or religion. One could not really go with both of them – at least not very far.

All that has changed dramatically in the past few decades.

The renewed sense of mystery introduced by modern physics and cosmology has had the effect of opening channels of communication to that other enduring mystery, religion... Science and theology no longer appear far apart. On the contrary, each may draw strength from the realm of the other... Science and religion might be closer than ever

---

We create change as we live out the experiences of our souls in the common acts of life.
Sue Monk Kidd

before to forming a continuum between those two towers of
human thought.
Robert Fripp[8]

It is ironic indeed that, while as Fripp says, the best of
science and religion form a 'continuum between those two
towers of human thought', it was also a lethal combination
of the worst of technology and fanatical religion that struck
down the Twin Towers of Manhattan. This is perhaps a
reminder, if we need it, that every new gleam of light that
dawns upon humanity also gives rise to a new shadow.

Traditional science and conventional religion have both
offered humankind pictures painted mainly in black and
white. Things were either 'true' or 'untrue'. Issues were
either 'right' or 'wrong'. And there tended to be a finality
about these judgments. Once decided, they were often
considered to be beyond debate, except among a small elite
of experts.

In the spirituality tradition, however, there has always
been a seam of subversion, suggesting more – *much more* –
beneath the surface of what conventional religious practice
would indicate. This subversive seam of thought and
experience belonged to the mystics, of all spiritual
traditions. While religion was laying down the rules and
dogmas, the mystics were speaking of the fundamental
unity and interrelatedness of all that is, of the impossibility
of getting our minds around the mystery of God, and of the
need to live with paradox, where nothing is black and

**It is in common searches and shared risks that new ideas are born,
that new visions reveal themselves and that new roads become visible.**
Henri Nouwen

white, and where every shade of grey is meaningful and necessary. The mystics have led those willing to follow, into a realm where, ultimately, nothing can be 'known' intellectually, and yet God's presence and power can be experienced and connected to.

Perhaps those very people who have followed the mystical path through the ages are smiling now to see our twenty-first century scientists finally catching up with them, and telling us that actually nothing is certain, nothing is predictable, everything is interconnected with everything else, and – yes – everything, ultimately, is mystery.

> *The opportunity of our time is to integrate science's understanding of the universe with more ancient intuitions concerning the meaning and destiny of the human...*
> *Science now enters its wisdom phase.*
> **Brian Swimme**[9]

And so two streams of human thought and reflection arrive at what looks like the same point by widely different routes.

> *In evolutionary terms, there are no ultimate facts about anything in life; there are no final answers nor perfect solutions. Indeed, contemporary science, itself dogmatically committed to factual, verifiable truth, verifies the fundamental uncertainty and unpredictability of all reality. And it is by entering more deeply into the unfolding story of*

**I realize that my faith and unbelief
are never far from each other.**

our universe – and all its constituent life forms – that we
encounter the truth that sets us free: to become the type of
people our creative God intends us to be.
Diairmuid Ó'Murchú[10]

When human minds from such very different disciplines
find themselves standing together on the edge of mystery,
there can be a new awakening. Each strand of exploration
brings its own baggage with it, however, and this can
generate suspicion and fear of the unknown questions that
every new answer brings in its wake. One fear is that it
may be dangerous to probe the mysteries of life. In some
respects we still live in a 'flat earth' mentality. We know
that we can safely sail our boats over the horizon without
falling off the globe, but we find it difficult to believe that
the same may be true in our spiritual exploring. Perhaps we
allow such fears more weight than they deserve.

If our knowledge is like a small island set in an ocean of
inexhaustible mystery, then the growth of the island does
not lessen either the size of the mystery or the sea; it just
increases the length of the shore a little. And perhaps we are
most human, most what we are called to be, when we have
one foot on that shore of what we know, and one foot in the
mysterious, unknown ocean. This is where the poet and the
painter stand, together with the best scientists and the
wisest theologians: exploring, probing, digging deeper; and
sometimes breaking through to a fresh realisation of truth.

Maybe it is exactly at the place where they touch each other
that the growing edge of my life is.
Henri Nouwen

Art, science and theology meet and flower at the boundary
of the known and the hidden. For all of us this is the dance,
not of certainty, but of faith.
Michael Mayne[11]

New understandings

The outworking of this new growth of consciousness, this
spiritual evolution, has already brought about great changes
in human attitudes and values, and has challenged us in
many ways to 'think outside the box'.

Each generation takes up this challenge in the light of
everything that preceding generations have achieved, and in
the shadow of all the mistakes they have made. There can
no longer be any question of any individual making the
journey into enlightenment alone. We are inextricably
interlinked with each other, and with all those who have
gone ahead of us, and those who will follow after. Each of
us has the choice, in all our dealings, as to whether our
own lives will help to take the human family a little closer
to God's Dream, or draw it a little further away from its
God-given destiny, into a downward spiral leading to
extinction.

As we collectively scale the mountain of explanation, each
generation stands firmly on the shoulders of the previous,
bravely reaching for the peak. Whether any of our
descendants will ever take in the view from the summit and

There's no great answer to everything. There's only
a developing process of which we are a part,

gaze out on the vast and elegant universe with a
perspective of infinite clarity, we cannot predict. But as
each generation climbs a little higher, we realize Jacob
Bronowski's pronouncement that 'in every age there is
a turning point, a new way of seeing and asserting the
coherence of the world'.
Brian Greene[12]

One of the more positive changes in the mood of our
times is that we are becoming increasingly uncomfortable
with a lifestyle based solely on the values of a consumer
society, especially when the affluence we enjoy rides on the
backs of the poorest peoples of the world. There are clear
indications that more and more people, especially young
people, are seeking deeper ground on which to build their
lives.

It is, I am convinced, what many young people are seeking
whether they have the words or not: something to live for,
something to give their lives for. The illusory goals of
shopping and making money will not cut it with most
young people. Deep down they resent this trivialising of
their existence. Deep down they know what Thomas
Aquinas taught, that we are 'capax universi', capable of
the universe, and they want to know their place in it, their
dignity derived from it, and their responsibility to it.
Matthew Fox[13]

---

and we'll always be pushing at the rim of the universe.
Jeanette Winterson

These same young people, who are searching for their place in the universe, are also travelling widely around the globe. One effect of this is that we are, as a human family, becoming less parochial. To travel is to discover that human beings in other lands and cultures are also people with whom we can share our laughter and our tears, and that what we have in common is a great deal more than the sum of all our differences.

> *Do we really need to belong to one country or one culture? In our world, where distances are becoming less each day, it seems important to become less and less dependent on one place, one language, one culture, or one style of life, but to experience oneself as a member of the human family, belonging to God and free to be wherever we are called to be. I even wonder if the ability to be in so many places so quickly and so often is not an invitation to grow deeper in the spirit and let our identity be more rooted in God and less in the place in which we happen to be.*
> **Henri Nouwen**[14]

Our spiritual horizons, too, are being stretched beyond the limits that traditional religion can comfortably contain. Denominational affiliation now goes hand in hand with a much deeper awareness of the need for ecumenical and inter-faith dialogue than ever before. A sense of relationship with God, and the challenges that poses, can no longer be seen as a Sundays-only affair if Christians are to be true to

---

The tendency of life is to point us in the right direction.
Deepak Chopra

their calling. The Christian vision must catch light in the world of daily life, and sometimes this collapses the structures that conventional practice has erected and calls into question traditional clericalism and hierarchy. Far from being a phenomenon of our age, this kind of iconoclasm lies at the heart of the gospel.

Christ did not direct everyone into sacred buildings or structures, but rather he moved into the world, going to the people, healing their ailments, and binding their secular lives to the sacred. Those lives were then transformed by virtue of their new relationship with the sacred. The way of the future will be the way of the founder; not to expect the world to submit to clerical authority, but to transform the world by revealing the presence of God where it least expects to find it, in the everyday and the ordinary.
David Tacey[15]

For many seekers today, the image of God presented by conventional religion is quite simply too small. To dismiss this often unspoken protest as 'secularism' is a great mistake. The world is very far from secular. Human beings are fundamentally deeply spiritual beings, and this heart-current of spiritual longing has never been more apparent than it is today.

The human world of today has not grown cold, but is ardently searching for a God proportionate to the new

---

All that I have written seems like straw to me.
Thomas Aquinas (And after that he wrote no more.)

dimensions of a Universe whose appearance has completely
revolutionised the scale of our faculty of worship...
Teilhard de Chardin[16]

Breakdown, breakthrough

And yet, in spite of all these positive movements, we still
pick up our newspapers and switch on our TV sets and
hear, on a daily basis, of apparently insuperable problems
in our streets, communities and nations. We hear of very
young children committing violent acts against each other.
We see our teenagers in the grip of a drug culture. We
know that injustice, and exploitation run through all our
institutions and corporations like a toxic stream, and we
feel helpless to change things. Is our civilization really
breaking down?

It has been wisely observed that when a new and
powerful stream breaks forth from a mountainside, it brings
a new source of water to quench our inner longing, but also
a great deal of rubble and silt in its wake. It isn't hard to see
the evidence of this deluge all around us. What is harder is
to detect where the life-giving stream is flowing in the midst
of it. Can we believe that the chaos that surrounds us is
actually a creative one?

When the old order collapses into disarray, as is happening
extensively today, the ensuing chaos has a strange sense of
creativity, a type of quantum leap that defies disintegration.

The commitment of faith is a response to a vision of goodness
whose attraction, once seen, is irresistible.
Keith Ward

It is a transition for which there is no known rationale other than that mysterious spiritual transformation that Christians call Resurrection.
Diarmuid O'Murchú[17]

It isn't easy to hold this possibility in mind when you are struggling to survive in the chaos. It wasn't easy to keep it in mind at the foot of the cross on Golgotha, and yet the fact of Calvary is a statement of absolute faith that what seems like total breakdown can be the beginning of a breakthrough we would never have imagined possible.

Sometimes this breakthrough comes precisely as a result of the conflict of intractable oppositions, both in our personal experience and in the wider world. To live in the tension of paradox may be to live on the brink of a new creation.

The opposite of a true statement is a false statement, the opposite of a profound truth can be another profound truth. The poles of a paradox are like the poles of a battery: hold them together, and they generate the energy of life; pull them apart, and the current stops flowing. When we separate any of the profound paired truths of our lives, both poles become lifeless spectres of themselves – and we become lifeless as well.
Niels Bohr, Nobel Prize-winning physicist[18]

We are closer to God when we are asking questions than when we think we have the answers.
Rabbi Abraham Joshua Heschel

There are many images and metaphors that humankind has woven to express this feeling of being in a state of conflict and chaos that we can only trust to be creative through an act of faith. We can picture ourselves as the broken threads in the weaving of some greater picture that we cannot ourselves envisage.

> *Every story is a luminous thread that becomes part of a larger fabric, a fabric we are weaving together for the whole world, and this fabric is a thing of immense importance and beauty.*
> **Sue Monk Kidd[19]**

We can see ourselves as living in a dangerous and messy building site, in process of being shaped into something only the architect can see.

> *Our earlier lives aren't wrong, they are just pre-construction, that's all. Our lives are meant to unfold, to evolve and that's good. The only wrong thing, perhaps, is permanently hesitating on the verge of courage, which would prevent this process from taking place.*
> **Sue Monk Kidd[20]**

God can, indeed, seem more intent on destroying our certainties than in shoring them up. While we strive to encapsulate our faith in creeds and dogmas, God, and life, continually bring us face to face with new experiences and

---

What power on earth has ever succeeded in arresting the growth of an idea or a passion, once they have taken shape?
Teilhard de Chardin

challenges that take us beyond the known and the understood. We struggle, and maybe we resist, but if we allow God to surprise us, we grow in the process.

The Bible is one long story about how God demolishes human beliefs in order to clear space for faith. Ask Abraham and Sarah, ask Elijah and Paul. Ask anyone who was ever granted intimacy with God. The moment you think you have the formula worked out, God changes the equation...

The Bible is full of stories about how our beliefs trip us up. So are our own lives. While most of us have acquired some useful maps for the journey (which include the teachings of both science and religion), very few of those maps are in mint condition. Instead they have scribbles all over them: dotted lines for the shortcuts we have found, a circled area where blueberries grow all summer, a skull and crossbones over the well that has dried up. Our maps are always under revision. Whether the subject is science or religion, our beliefs are always challenged by our experience, which begs us never to put the lid on truth.
Barbara Brown Taylor[21]

One of the results of living with surprises is that we learn to be who we are in whatever circumstances surround us. I remember the day I first met the evening primrose! The evening primrose is a remarkable flower, that literally pops into blossom about half an hour before dusk. If you watch,

---

Tradition is having a baby, not wearing your father's hat.
Attributed to Picasso

you will see the sheath surrounding the flower bud open up dramatically before your eyes, and you will be able to watch the joyful burst with which the clear yellow flower unfolds itself, like a butterfly emerging from the chrysalis and spreading its wings to dry. It's a bit like watching a speeded-up nature film. The flower emerges, fresh into the night air, in just a few short, fascinating minutes. But the other astonishing fact about the evening primrose is that it only has around twenty-four hours to live. The next evening, after its triumphant emergence into the world, it will be hanging limp on the stem.

Whenever I see an evening primrose I feel I want to wish it a really good day for its brief sojourn on earth. For some of them the day ahead will be bright and sunny. For others it will be rain-soaked and drab. And that's true for people too. Some of our lives will be lived in the sun, with little to trouble us. For others, life will be one long struggle. We have as little control over our circumstances, in some respects, as the hapless evening primrose. One little life is all we get, and whatever hand it deals us, we are invited to make something of it. The evening primroses manage to fulfil their role in creation whatever the weather. They enrich the brief hours of their life for all creation, by their presence in it, and then they pass on their unique seed of life to the future. Can we do the same?

A series of twisted relationships has taught us to fear no one. A plethora of failures has taught us that nothing can

---

It is only when the dragonfly larva sheds her skin that she sees the Sun in all his glory.
From the Epic of Gilgamesh

really destroy us. A streak of great good luck has
demonstrated as clearly as our errors how really little
control we can claim over anything. It is age that teaches
us how, freed from false guarantees about tomorrow, we
can finally let go and live life well today.
Joan Chittister[22]

Trusting the mystery

God is nothing if not elusive! I like the description of the
spiritual quest as being like trying to take a close-up photo
of the horizon. Frustrating in the extreme – and yet the
most compelling desire we will ever know, and the quest
that keeps us continually moving on, and discovering that
in the moving and the reaching out we are growing daily
closer to who we truly are.

Just as the branches of a tree grow through reaching
outwards and upwards towards the light, and its roots
grow by reaching downwards for the water and
nourishment they crave, so we too grow by stretching.
To allow ourselves to be stretched means that we must
acknowledge that God is a Mystery, and that God is to
be discovered in our uncertainty more than in our
certainty.

The place of expansion is always on the border. On the
edge. If we're going to turn from restrictive God-talk…
if we're going to become whole, we have to go to the edge…

A peace activist was asked 'What are you hoping to achieve?'
She replied: 'We are trying to prevent the seventh war from now.'

Now for the paradox. When we get there, we find it's not the edge at all. No, the edge is still further in the distance. The thing is, you can never overtake the Divine.
Sue Monk Kidd[23]

We can never overtake the Divine. We can never get our close-up photo of the horizon. But in the quest we have a unique opportunity to discover not only who we are, but where our destiny lies in the scheme of things.

God, meanwhile, playfully conceals Godself in the places we think are too familiar to bother looking – in our own experience.

One of the lovely things about the Bible is that God is always appearing in the most unexpected places, and that happens both in the Old Testament and the New Testament. So the obvious places where God is to be found – in the synagogues or in the churches, even in the scrolls of the law – are not just where God is found. God is found among the ordinary people – at sea, on boats, in the market place, with the whores, with the sinners – so that God is fugitive from our authority. You know, we try to contain God and God always says, 'I'm not here, I'm somewhere else.'
Jeanette Winterson[24]

While we cannot, of course, ever arrive at 'the horizon', we are nevertheless called, as human beings, to trust that we have a role to fulfil in the ongoing transformation of

The future belongs to those who believe in the beauty of their dreams.
Teilhard de Chardin

planet earth into the kingdom of God. This destiny has been ours from the earliest beginnings, and each generation takes up the quest from those who have gone ahead. To make this quest in faith, we need to trust that God is indeed a God of love who is constantly seeking to draw the more life-giving outcome from all our circumstances and responses.

> We must feel that we are supported by that same power that brought the Earth into being, that power that spun the galaxies into space, that lit the sun and brought the moon into its orbit. That is the power by which living forms grew up out of the Earth and came to a special mode of reflexive consciousness in the human. This is the force that brought us through more than a million years of wandering as hunters and gatherers; this is that same vitality that led to the establishment of our cities and inspired the thinkers, artists and poets of the ages. Those same forces are still present; indeed, we might feel their impact at this time and understand that we are not isolated in the chill of space with the burden of the future upon us and without the aid of any other power.
>
> **Thomas Berry**[25]

To embark upon this quest is to let go of our own power agendas and need for absolute certainty. There is no answer book, and there never could be, because the secret of growth is the working out for ourselves, with God's

---

Wisdom does not grow old; it is always one day old. Wisdom is as old as creation and as young as a newborn babe.
John Martin Sahajananda

guidance and grace, what is the more human, the more life-giving, the more Christ-like response to any given situation.

The Christian gospel is not about producing QED answers to life's problems, but about encountering mystery. Faith, like hope, is an attitude of the heart, a changed orientation of the spirit. It is to trust that love is at the heart of the Mystery for whom the English name is 'God'. And to do so in the face of the undeniable confusion, uncertainty and doubt which remain a natural part of all our lives.
Michael Mayne[26]

The big picture takes over – alluring and exciting, but so petrifying for those locked into the ideology of power and control. Power belongs to a small world, often unable to see or appreciate the larger reality that embraces all. And it is on this larger scale that the revolution of consciousness and its evolutionary expansion are happening in our time.

The question is this: Are there enough wise and free people poised to seize the moment? In other words: Can we make the shift in consciousness that could make a substantial difference?
Diairmuid Ó'Murchú[27]

Do we have to be mystics to embrace this challenge? The gospel narratives recording the way Jesus of Nazareth moved through his contemporary world certainly don't indicate that he asked for any kind of special qualifications

---

The best criticism of the bad is the practice of the better.
Richard Rohr

from those who would learn from him. Quite the reverse.
He urged us to 'become as little children', to let go the
need for certainty and live by trust, always open to God's
surprises. Children don't have any sense of a 'destination' –
they simply live life moment by moment, just as it comes,
and it is during these carefree years that they do most of
their growing. In this regard they are like the saints.

> *I don't think mystics are set apart from ordinary people.
> They are just better quantum navigators. They journey into
> a transition zone closer to God, and while we might visit
> there for a few moments of joy, at most a few days, saints
> and mystics have found the secret of remaining there far
> longer. Instead of wondering about the mystery of life, a
> saint lives it.*
> **Deepak Chopra**[28]

Living into tomorrow

There is a story told by Francis Dewar about Michelangelo:

> *He was sweating as he manoeuvred a large rock down the
> street. One onlooker, standing idly at a doorway, asked why
> on earth he was expending so much effort shifting a lump of
> stone. 'Because', came the reply, 'there is an angel in there
> that wants to walk free.'*
> **Francis Dewar**[29]

The glory of God is the human person fully alive.
St Irenaeus

Living into tomorrow is a bit like that. We believe and we trust that there is something eternal hidden in the rough stone of our present experience of life. To be part of the adventure of releasing that eternal reality is to embrace our destiny as human beings striving for transcendence. But the effort is very costly. It will demand every ounce of our energy, all our commitment, and a large measure of trust. We will sweat a lot, and we may never see any 'success' for our labours. We will be the sowers of seeds for a harvest we may never experience.

It is too painfully true: the business of changing the world one heart at a time requires the courage of the mountain climber who goes alone where none have been to plant the flag of human possibility that no one sought.

It is not an easy thing, this sowing the seeds of the next human frontier, the next layer of moral imagination in the always unfinished and frustratingly ongoing process of creation. Those who need to know success need not apply. Sowing is for people of conscience only, for people who cannot live with themselves if they live on a lesser level than they know in their hearts life is really meant to be. They deal with ridicule; they feel rejection; they know the dailiness of defeat...

Planting ideas and questions and possibilities in the human psyche, like planting the fields of the desert, is at best a desolate and potentially devastating moral duty. After all, the sowers may never know whether their lives really

---

We are earth that has come to consciousness.
Richard Rohr

had any value at all. 'If you expect to see the results of your work,' the Talmud teaches, 'you have simply not asked a big enough question.'
Joan Chittister[30]

Oscar Romero, who lost his life at the hands of assassins, while celebrating Mass in San Salvador, was an outstanding example of one who labours for what he describes as 'a future not our own'.

*We accomplish in our life time only a tiny fraction
of the magnificent enterprise that is God's work.
Nothing we do is complete, which is another way of saying
that the Kingdom always lies beyond us.
No statement says all that could be said.
No prayer fully expresses our faith.
No confession brings perfection.
No pastoral visit brings wholeness.
No programme accomplishes the Church's mission.
No set of goals and objectives includes everything.
That is what we are about:
We plant the seeds that one day will grow.
We water seeds already planted,
knowing that they hold promise.
We lay foundations that will need further development.
We provide yeast that produces effects far beyond our capabilities.
We cannot do everything, and there is a sense of liberation in
realising that.*

**We might have to spend a whole lifetime walking in darkness,
recalling the little we've experienced the light.**
Richard Rohr

This enables us to do something and to do it very well.
It may be incomplete, but it is a beginning,
a step along the way,
an opportunity for the Lord's grace to enter and do the rest;
but that is the difference
between the master builder and the worker.
We are the workers, not the master builders.
Ministers, not messiahs.
We are prophets of a future not our own.
Oscar Romero

We can, of course, choose not to put on this mantle of prophecy, and remain instead in our accustomed comfort zones. Sometimes we do this because we are afraid of commitment, but often it happens because we simply do not realize who we are, in God's sight, and who we have the potential to become. This is true for each of us personally, just as for all of us, the human family on earth. We are called to transcendence. Will we hear that still, small voice within us, and if we hear it, will we trust it? Will we follow where it leads? Is our heart's journey the soaring of the eagle, or the scrabbling of the chicken...?

A farmer brought home a chick from an eagles' eyrie. Not quite knowing what to do with it, he put it in a chicken run, where it grew up with the chickens. One day a passing traveller saw it, and commented on its presence. 'It's a chicken,' said the farmer. 'Not so,' said the traveller, 'it's an

---

eagle.' And he took it on his wrist and spoke to the great
bird. 'You're an eagle,' he said. 'Fly!' But the eagle looked
down at the chickens in the run, hopped down and pecked
with them. 'You see,' said the farmer, 'I told you so. It's a
chicken.'

For the next week the traveller called each day and
brought such food as is proper to an eagle, raw meat and
flesh. Slowly the bird's strength began to revive.

So again the traveller took the bird on his wrist and
spoke to it: 'You're an eagle,' he said. 'Fly!' And the great
bird stretched his wings, but when he saw the chickens in
the run, he hopped down and scratched with them, 'You're
wasting your time,' said the farmer, 'I told you. It's a
chicken.'

Next morning, while it was still dark, the traveller
returned, and taking the bird on his wrist he walked a little
way into the bush. As the morning sun rose and tipped with
a golden light the great crag where the eagles' eyrie was
built, he lifted the bird and pointed to the mountain top:
'You're an eagle,' he said. 'Fly!' And the great bird looked
up to the top of the crag, stretched his wings and flew,
round and round and round... until he vanished in the sky.
James Aggrey[31]

God calls us to believe in our inner eagle, as
individuals and as the whole human family. To fly, we
must trust that we are going somewhere, which, in turn,
means that we have not yet arrived. To fly means to live

We're creating the future every day, by what we choose to do.
Margaret Wheatley

each moment, with its risks and its glory, and to receive the seeds of life and love from all our yesterdays, and to let the fruits of our own experience be the gift we pass on to tomorrow.

I will not live an unlived life,
I will not go in fear
Of falling or catching fire.
I choose to inhabit my days,
To allow my living to open to me,
To make me less afraid,
More accessible,
To loosen my heart
Until it becomes a wing,
A torch, a promise.
I choose to risk my significance:
To live.
So that which came to me as a seed,
Goes to the next as a blossom,
And that which came to me as a blossom
Goes on as a fruit.
Davina Marcova[32]

May our own hearts be always open to receive the seeds of wisdom, for they are the gift of God.

May the seeds break into blossom, and may the blossom ripen into fruit.

The way of wisdom is unending. We have roamed some

Tell me what you plan to do with your one wild, precious life?
Mary Oliver

of its landscapes and glimpsed some of its treasures. I bid you farewell in the words of Kahlil Gibran:

I beg you to forgive me for beginning a story that I cannot end. But the end is not yet upon my lips. It is still a love song in the wind.
Kahlil Gibran[33]

Give thanks for unknown blessings already on their way.
Native American saying

References

Original Wisdom

1. Matthew Fox, *Original Blessings*, Santa Fe, Bear & Company, 1983.

2. Brian Swimme and Thomas Berry, *The Universe Story*, HarperSanFrancisco, 1994.

3. Augustine of Hippo quoted in Martin Rees, *Just Six Numbers*, London, Weidenfeld & Nicholson, 1999.

4. Gerald Schroeder, *The Hidden Face of God*, New York, The Free Press, 2001.

5. Robert Fripp, *Let There Be Life*, New Jersey, Hidden Spring, 2001.

6. Matthew Fox, *Original Blessings*, op.cit.

7. Martin Rees, *Just Six Numbers*, op.cit.

8. Alister McGrath, *Glimpsing the Face of God*, Oxford, Lion Publishing, 2003.

9. Brian Swimme and Thomas Berry, *The Universe Story*, op.cit.

10. Matthew Fox, *One River, Many Wells*, Dublin, Gateway, 2000.

11. Barbara Brown Taylor, *The Luminous Web*, Cambridge, Massachussets, Cowley Publications, 2000.

12. Ralph Wright, OSB, *Leaves of Water*, St Louis, Missouri, St Louis Abbey Press, 1997.

13. David Tacey, *The Spirituality Revolution*, New York, Brunner-Routledge, 2004.

14. Sue Monk Kidd, *The Dance of the Dissident Daughter*, HarperSanFrancisco, 2002.

15. Barbara Brown Taylor, *The Luminous Web*, op. cit.

16. Annie Dillard, *Pilgrim at Tinker Creek*, London, Picador, 1974.

17. Julian of Norwich, *Revelations of Divine Love*, translated by Clifton Wolters, London, Penguin, 1966.

18. Matthew Fox, *One River, Many Wells*, op. cit.

19. Thomas Berry, *The Great Work*, New York, Bell Tower, 1999.

20. Extract from Ronald Rohlheiser, 3rd Internet reflection for Lent 2005

21. Barbara Brown Taylor, *The Luminous Web*, op. cit.

Natural Wisdom

1. Paul Davies in *Devout Sceptics*, ed. by Bel Mooney, Hodder and Stoughton, 2003.

2. Rabbi David W. Nelson, *Judaism, Physics and God*, Woodstock, Vermont, Jewish Lights Publishing, 2005.

3. Barbara Brown Taylor, *The Luminous Web*, Cambridge, Mass, Cowley Publications, 2000.

4. Michael Mayne, *This Sunrise of Wonder*, London, Fount Paperbacks, 1995.

5. Deepak Chopra, *Unconditional Life*, Bantam USA.

6. Gerald Schroeder, *The Hidden Face of God*, New York, The Free Press, 2001.

7. Thich Nhat Hanh, *Going Home*, New York, Riverhead Books, 1999.

8. Brian Swimme, *The Hidden Heart of the Cosmos*, Maryknoll, New York, Orbis Books, 1996.

9. William Wordsworth, 'Lines composed a few miles above Tintern Abbey, 1798'.

10. Keith Ward, *God – A Guide for the Perplexed*, Oxford, Oneworld Publications, 2003.

11. Annie Dillard, *Pilgrim at Tinker Creek*, London, Picador, 1974.

12. Joseph Mary Plunkett, 'I see his blood upon the rose', 1916.

13. Filipino reflection, quoted in Matthew Fox, *One River, Many Wells*, Dublin, Gateway, 2000.

14. James Lovelock, *Gaia – A New Look at Life on Earth*, Oxford University Press, 2000.

15. Thomas Berry, *The Great Work*, New York, Bell Tower, 1999.

16. Philip Yancey, from 'Penguins on Parade' in *Australian Stories for the Soul*, Sydney, Strand Publishing, 2001.

17. Robert Fripp, *Let There Be Life*, New Jersey, Hidden Spring, 2001.

18. Diairmuid Ó'Murchú, *Evolutionary Faith*, Maryknoll, New York, Orbis Books, 2002.

19. Augustine of Hippo quoted in Robert Fripp, *Let There Be Life*, op. cit.

20. Gerd Thiessen, *The Shadow of the Galilean*, London, SCM Press, 1987.

21. Nikos Kazantzakis, *Zorba the Greek*, Bruno Cassirer, 1959.

22. Bede Griffiths, *Return to the Centre*, London, Collins, 1976.

23. Antoine de Saint-Exupéry, *The Little Prince*, London, Pan Books, 1974.

Indigenous Wisdom

1. Brian Swimme, *The Hidden Heart of the Cosmos*, Maryknoll, New York, Orbis Books, 1996.

2. Marlo Morgan, *Mutant Message from Forever*, London, Thorsons, 2000.

3. Fran Dancing Feather and Rita Robinson, *Exploring Native American Wisdom*, Franklin Lakes, New Jersey, Career Press, 2003.

4. Esther de Waal, *The Celtic Way of Prayer*, London, Hodder & Stoughton, 1996.

5. Fran Dancing Feather and Rita Robinson, *Exploring Native American Wisdom*, op. cit.

6. Chief Seathl, *Chief Seathl's Testament*, Mt Saint Bernard Abbey, Coalville, Leicester, Saint Bernard Press.

7. Quoted in Francis Dewar, *Invitations*, London, SPCK, 1996.

8. Matthew Fox, *One River, Many Wells*, Dublin, Gateway, 2000.

9. Brooke Medicine Eagle (Crow Indian), quoted in *The Little Book of Native American Wisdom*, Element Books Ltd.

10. Grandfather David Monongye, Hopi, quoted in *The Little Book of Native American Wisdom*, op. cit.

11. Marlo Morgan, *Mutant Message from Forever*, op.cit.

12. Fran Dancing Feather and Rita Robinson, *Exploring Native American Wisdom*, op. cit.

13. Bede Griffiths, *Return to the Centre*, London, Collins, 1976.

14. Kenneth Kaunda 'Humanism and Community in Africa' in *African Christian Spirituality*, Maryknoll, New York, Orbis Books, 1978.

15. Oren Lyons, *Faithkeeper*, Onondaga Nation, Earth Day 1993 Pledge.

16. Aylward Shorter, *African Christian Spirituality*, op. cit.

17. Diairmuid Ó'Murchú, *Evolutionary Faith*, Maryknoll, New York, Orbis Books, 2002.

18. Thomas Berry, *The Great Work*, New York, Bell Tower, 1999.

19. Esther de Waal, *The Celtic Way of Prayer*, op. cit.

20. Esther de Waal, *A World Made Whole*, London, Fount Paperbacks, 1991.

21. Marlo Morgan, *Mutant Message Down Under*, op. cit.

22. Matthew Fox, *One River, Many Wells*, op. cit.

23. Michael Smith, from *Helen House News*, Spring 1995.

24. Brian Swimme, *The Hidden Heart of the Cosmos*, op. cit.

25. Brian McClorry SJ, unpublished poem, reproduced by permission of the author.

Desert Wisdom

1. Alan Jamieson, *Journeying in Faith*, London, SPCK, 2004.

2. Ralph Wright OSB, *Leaves of Water*, St Louis, Missouri, St Louis Abbey Press, 1997.

3. Jim Cotter from *SPCK Book of Christian Prayers*, London, SPCK, 1995.

4. Kathleen Norris, 'The Aridity of Grace, & Other Comedies' from *Portland Magazine*.

5. Marie Therese Archambault, *A Retreat with Black Elk*, Cincinatti, Ohio, St Anthony Messenger Press, 1998.

6. Sheila Cassidy, *Audacity to Believe*, London, Fount Paperbacks, 1978.

7. Oswald Tilley, quoted in Brown, Malcolm and Shirley, *Christmas Truce*, New York, Hippocrene Books, 1984

8. Ylva Eggehorn, 'Stå stilla I smärtan' translated from the Swedish by Kerstin Eadie, quoted in Donald Eadie, *Grain in Winter*, Peterborough, Epworth Press, 1999.

9. Thomas Keneally, *Schindler's List*, Sceptre, 1994.

10. Viktor E. Frankl, *Man's Search for Meaning*, London, Rider, 2004.

11. Yann Martell, *Life of Pi*, Edinburgh, Cannongate Books, 2002.

12. May Sarton, from *Halfway to Silence*, W.W. Norton, 1980.

13. Lavinia Byrne, *Sharing the Vision*, London, SPCK, 1989.

14. Henri Nouwen, *The Wounded Healer*, London, Darton, Longman & Todd, 1994.

15. Desmond Tutu, *God Has a Dream*, London, Rider, 2004.

16. Etty Hillesum, *An Interrupted Life*, London, Persephone Books, 1999.

17. Brian Keenan, *An Evil Cradling*, London, Vintage, 1993.

18. Sheila Cassidy, *Audacity to Believe*, op. cit.

19. Jean Vanier, *Our Journey Home*, London, Hodder & Stoughton, 1997.

20. Brian Keenan, *An Evil Cradling*, op. cit.

21. Rainer Maria Rilke, 'Letters to a Young Poet'.

Guiding Wisdom

1. Patrick Kavanagh, from 'The Great Hunger', *Selected Poems*, London, Penguin Books, 1996.

2. *The Gift: Poems by Hafiz the Great Sufi Master*, translated by Daniel Ladinsky, New York, Arkana, 1999.

3. Alice Walker, *The Color Purple*, London, Phoenix, 2004.

4. John Martin Sahajananda, *You are the Light*, Alresford, Hants, O Books, 2003.

5. Gerard Hughes, *God, Where are You?*, London, Darton, Longman & Todd, 1997.

6. Kahlil Gibran, *Jesus the Son of Man*, London, Arkana, Penguin, 1928.

7. Michael Mayne, *This Sunrise of Wonder*, London, Fount Paperbacks, 1995.

8. Rainer Maria Rilke, *Book of Hours*, New York, Riverhead Books, 1996.

9. Brian Woodcock, from *This is the Day* (Iona Community) ed. by Neil Paynter, Glasgow, Wild Goose Publications, 2002.

10. Deepak Chopra, *How to know God*, London, Rider, 2000.

11. Keith Ward, *God – A Guide for the Perplexed*, Oxford, Oneworld Publications, 2003.

12. Diairmuid Ó'Murchú, *Reclaiming Spirituality*, Dublin, Gill & Macmillan Ltd, 1997.

13. Henri Nouwen, *Bread for the Journey*, London, Darton, Longman & Todd, 1996.

14. Isabel Allende, in *Devout Sceptics*, ed. by Bel Mooney, Hodder and Stoughton, 2003.

15. Melvyn Bragg, in *Devout Sceptics*, op. cit.

16. Donald Nicholl, *The Testing of Hearts*, London, Darton, Longman & Todd, 1998.

17. Satish Kumar, *You are Therefore I am*, Totnes, Devon, Green Books Ltd, 2002.

18. Isabel Allende in *Devout Sceptics* op. cit.

19. Henri Nouwen, *The Road to Daybreak*, London, Darton, Longman & Todd, 1997.

20. Neale Donald Walsch, *Tomorrow's God*, London, Hodder & Stoughton, 2004.

21. Anecdote recounted by Francis Dewar in *Invitations*, London, SPCK, 1996.

22. Thich Nhat Hanh, *Peace is Every Step*, London, Rider, 1995.

23. William Blake, 'Auguries of Innocence'.

24. Quoted in Francis Dewar, *Invitations*, op. cit.

25. Keith Ward, *God – A Guide for the Perplexed,* op. cit.

26. Deepak Chopra, *How to Know God*, op. cit.

27. Adrian B. Smith, *A Reason for Living and Hoping*, London, St Paul's Publishing, 2002.

28. Richard Rohr, *Everything Belongs*, New York, Crossroad Publishing, 1999.

29. Arthur James, 'Our highest truths are but half-truths'.

30. C. Day Lewis, 'Walking Away'.

31. Henri Nouwen, *Bread for the Journey*, op. cit.

32. Rabindranath Tagore 'The Gardener', translated from a German version by Margaret Silf.

Life Wisdom

1. Patrick Kavanagh, from 'To Hell with Commonsense', *Selected Poems*, London, Penguin, 1996.

2. Emily Dickinson, 'Experience'.

3. Sue Monk Kidd, *The Secret Life of Bees*, New York, Penguin, 2002.

4. Bruce Lee, *Striking Thoughts*, Boston, Massachusetts, Turtle Publishing, 2000.

5. Robert Kirschner, *Divine Things*, New York, Crossroad Publishing, 2001.

6. Mary Wainwright, 'Our Reason for Existence' from a newsletter, Cygnus Books 20 September, 2004.

7. Keith Ward, *God – A Guide for the Perplexed*, Oxford, Oneworld Publications, 2003.

8. Mitch Albom, *Five People You Meet in Heaven*, St Ives, Little, Brown, 2003.

9. Joan Chittister, *There is a Season*, Maryknoll, New York, Orbis Books, 1995.

10. Leo Tolstoy in *Leo Tolstoy: A Calendar of Wisdom*, Hodder & Stoughton, 1997.

11. Kahlil Gibran, *The Prophet*, Pan Books, 1991.

12. Peter Lomas, 'True and False Experience', re-printed in Francis Dewar, *Live for a Change*, London, Darton, Longman & Todd, 1988.

13. Louis de Bernières, *Captain Corelli's Mandolin*, London, Mandarin Paperbacks, 1995.

14. Michael Mayne, *Learning to Dance*, London, Darton, Longman & Todd, 2001.

15. Kahlil Gibran, *The Prophet*, op. cit.

16. Thornton Wilder, *The Bridge of San Luis Rey*, London, Penguin Classics, 2000.

17. Brian Keenan, *An Evil Cradling*, London, Vintage, 1993.

18. Bruce Lee, *Striking Thoughts*, op. cit.

19. Robert Kirschner, *Divine Things*, op. cit.

20. David Tacey, *The Spirituality Revolution*, New York, Brunner-Routledge, 2004.

21. Pamela Hussey, 'Women in El Salvador's Church', *Free from Fear*, London, Catholic Institute for International Relations, 1989.

22. Antoine de Saint-Exupéry, *The Little Prince*, London, Pan Books, 1974.

23. Mitch Albom, *Five People You Meet in Heaven*, op. cit.

24. Yann Martell, *Life of Pi*, Edinburgh, Cannongate Books, 2002.

25. John Ballard, 'The Man with a Bag of Nails'.

26. Harper Lee, *To Kill a Mockingbird*, London, Vintage, 2004.

27. Jean Vanier, *Our Journey Home*, London, Hodder & Stoughton, 1997.

28. Helder Camara, 'Pilgrim'.

29. Kahlil Gibran, *The Prophet*, op. cit.

30. Robert Kirschner, *Divine Things*, op. cit.

31. Ruth Burrows, *Living in Mystery*, London, Sheed & Wardm 1996.

Unfolding Wisdom

1. Brian Swimme, *The Hidden Heart of the Cosmos*, Maryknoll, New York, Orbis Books, 1996.

2. Teilhard de Chardin, 'On the Probable Existence Ahead', 1950, reproduced in *The Future of Man*, New York, Image Books, Doubleday, 1959.

3. John Main OSB, *Word into Silence*, London, Darton, Longman & Todd, 1980.

4. Thomas Berry, *The Great Work*, New York, Bell Tower, 1999.

5. Bede Griffiths, *Return to the Centre*, London, Collins, 1976.

6. Teilhard de Chardin 'The Evolution of Christianity' in 'Toward the Future' in *Pierre Teilhard de Chardin, Selected Writings*, Ursula King, Maryknoll, New York, Orbis Books, 1999.

7. Diairmuid Ó'Murchú, *Religion in Exile*, Dublin, Gill & Macmillan, 2000.

8. Robert Fripp, *Let There Be Life*, New Jersey, Hidden Spring, 2001.

9. Brian Swimme, *The Hidden Heart of the Cosmos*, op. cit.

10. Diairmuid Ó'Murchú, *Religion in Exile*, op. cit.

11. Michael Mayne, *Learning to Dance*, London, Darton, Longman & Todd, 2001.

12. Brian Greene, *The Elegant Universe*, Vintage, 2000.

13. Matthew Fox, *One River, Many Wells*, Dublin, Gateway, 2000.

14. Henri Nouwen, *The Road to Daybreak*, London, Darton, Longman & Todd, 1997.

15. David Tacey, *The Spirituality Revolution*, New York, Brunner-Routledge, 2004.

16. Teilhard de Chardin, 'On the Probable Existence Ahead', op. cit.

17. Diarmuid O'Murchú, *Our World in Transition*, Lewes, Sussex, The Book Guild Ltd, 1992.

18. Niels Bohr quoted in Parker Palmer, *The Courage to Teach*, San Francisco, Jossey Bass, 1998.

19. Sue Monk Kidd, *The Dance of the Dissident Daughter*, HarperSanFrancisco, 2002.

20. Sue Monk Kidd, *The Dance of the Dissident Daughter*, op. cit.

21. Barbara Brown Taylor, *The Luminous Web*, Cambridge, Mass, Cowley Publications, 2000.

22. Joan Chittister, *There is a Season*, Maryknoll, New York, Orbis Books, 1995.

23. Sue Monk Kidd, *The Dance of the Dissident Daughter*, op. cit.

24. Jeanette Winterson in *Devout Sceptics*, ed. by Bel Mooney, Hodder and Stoughton, 2003.

25. Thomas Berry, *The Great Work*, New York, Bell Tower, 1999.

26. Michael Mayne, *Learning to Dance*, op. cit.

27. Diairmuid Ó'Murchú, *Evolutionary Faith*, Maryknoll, New York, Orbis Books, 2002.

28. Deepak Chopra, *How to Know God*, London, Rider, 2000.

29. Francis Dewar in *Invitations*, London, SPCK, 1996.

30. Joan Chittister, *There is a Season*, op. cit.

31. Fable told by James Aggrey, quoted in Francis Dewar, *Invitations*, op. cit.

32. Davina Marcova, quoted in Alan Jamieson, *Journeying in Faith*, London, SPCK, 2004.

33. Kahlil Gibran, *Jesus the Son of Man*, London, Arkana, Penguin, 1928.

Text Acknowledgments

pp. 25–26, 87 'It Took All the Chemistry' and 'Warshock', from *Leaves of Water* by Fr Ralph Wright O.S.B., published by Saint Louis Abbey. Reprinted with permission.

pp. 59, 61, 62–63, 66, 67, 77, 79 Extracts from *Mutant Message from Forever* by Marlo Morgan, published by Thorsons 2000.

p. 81–82. Poem by Brian McClorry. Reprinted with the author's permission.

p. 83 Excerpt from *Rilke's Book of Hours: Love Poems to God* by Rainer Maria Rilke, translated by Anita Barrows and Joanna Macy. Copyright © 1996 by Anita Barrows and Joanna Macy. Reprinted by permission of the author.

pp. 87, 101. Extract from 'Halfway to Silence' from *Of the Muse* by May Sarton. Reprinted by the permission of Russell & Volkening as agents for the author. Copyright © 1979 by May Sarton.

pp. 88–89 Jim Cotter (based on a prayer by George Appleton), Waymarks: Cairns for a Journey, Cairns Publications 2001.

pp. 112, 141, 148. The lines of Patrick Kavanagh from 'The Great Hunger', 'To Hell with Commonsense' and 'To Be Dead' are reprinted from *Collected Poems*, edited by Antoinette Quin (Allem Lane, 2004), by kind permission of the Trustees of the Estate of the late Katherine B. Kavanagh, through the Jonathan Williams Literary Agency.

p. 113 'Tired of Speaking Sweetly' from *The Gift* by Daniel Ladinsky. Copyright © 1999 by Daniel Ladinsky. Reprinted by permission of the author.

p. 117 Extract from 'The Book of Pilgrimage' from *Selected Works Volume II* by Rainer Maria Rilke and translated by J. B. Leishman and published by The Hogarth Press. Reprinted by permission of The Random House Group Ltd and Insel Verlag.

pp. 125–127 Extract from 'The testing of Hearts' by Donald Nicholls. Copyright © 1989 Donald Nichols, published by DLT in 1998.

pp. 137 Extract from 'Walking Away' by C. Day Lewis. Reprinted with permission from PFD Group Ltd.

p. 144 'The Reason for Your Existence' by Mary Wainwright. Reprinted with the author's permission.

pp. 148–151 Extract from 'True and False Experience' by Peter Lomas. Reprinted with permission from PFD Group Ltd.

pp. 160–161 Extract from 'The Man With a Bag of Nails' by John Ballard. Reprinted with permissions from Pickpocket Books.

p. 194 Excerpted from 'I will Not Die an Unlived Life' by Dawna Markova, with permission of Conari Press, imprint of Red Wheel/Wesier, Boston, MA and York Beach, ME.

Also available from Lion Hudson:

ONE HUNDRED WISDOM STORIES
Margaret Silf

This vivid and varied collection of stories with a spiritual message is gathered together by Margaret Silf from a wide range of time periods and cultures around the world. Stories can be a powerful means of communication; each of these tales has at its heart a spiritual message that reflects Christian values, which means that they can be read at different levels. They are ideal for personal use and enjoyment, and will also be a valuable resource for church leaders and school teachers.

'A beautifully packaged and highly-readable anthology of stories from different eras and cultures chosen to reflect Christian values that will appeal to people of all backgrounds.'
The Bookseller

ISBN: 0 7459 5082 5

SACRED SPACES
Margaret Silf

For the Celts, certain places were sacred – places where the divide
between visible and invisible was very thin, where the presence of
the spiritual was almost palpable. They revered such 'thin places' as
'sacred space'. In this book, retreat leader and writer Margaret Silf
introduces seven traditional sacred spaces: the Infinite Knot; the Celtic
Cross; Hilltops; Wells; Groves and Springs; Thresholds and Crossing
Places and Boundaries.

Each chapter leads us into a deeper reflection on what one
of these sacred spaces can mean in our own lives, drawing on
imaginative retellings of sacred stories from scripture and legend
to help us find the thread of our own story.

'Beautifully produced with breathtaking photographs and glossy pages.
Margaret Silf writes in a very accessible way. [Sacred Spaces] could
appeal to a wide spectrum of spiritual seekers.'
Spirituality

ISBN: 0 7459 5113 9

All Lion Books are available from your local bookshop, or can be ordered via our website or from Marston Book Services. For a free catalogue, showing the complete list of titles available, please contact:

Customer Services
Marston Book Services
PO Box 269
Abingdon
Oxon
OX14 4YN

Tel: 01235 465500
Fax: 01235 465555

Our website can be found at:
www.lionhudson.com